The Townhouse Gardener

The Townhouse Gardener

Sherry Mitchell

Illustrated by
Elaine Butt

EPM Publications, Inc.
McLean, Virginia

For my girlfriends,
on (and near) Surrey House Way,
who never let me down.

I love you all like sisters.

Library of Congress Cataloging-in-Publication Data

Mitchell, Sherry.
  The townhouse gardener: distinctive landscape designs for small
gardens in the Mid-Atlantic region / Sherry Mitchell.
     p. cm.
  Includes bibliographical references (p.) and index.
  ISBN 1-889324-09-4
   1. Gardens—Middle Atlantic States—Design. 2. Landscape
gardening—Middle Atlantic States. 3. Row houses—Middle Atlantic
States. I. Title
SB473.M626 1998
712'.6'0974—dc21   97-49065
                     CIP

EPM Publications, Inc., 1003 Turkey Run Road
 McLean, VA 22101
Printed in the United States of America

First Printing, February, 1998

Cover and book design by Tom Huestis
Illustrations © 1998 by Elaine Butt

Contents

The Joy
of
Small Spaces

According to the National Association of Home Builders, townhouses comprise 10 percent of all new homes built in the United States. That percentage increases dramatically to almost 40 percent around major northeastern cities such as Washington D.C., Philadelphia and New York where land is at a premium. This translates into thousands of tiny yards—yards that are just begging to be turned into beautiful garden sanctuaries.

The first garden I ever owned was a townhouse garden. Having come from a gardening family, and owning my own landscape firm, I had spent my entire life gardening, but had never gardened on my own land before marrying and moving to an end-unit townhouse in Fairfax, Virginia. Through trial and error, I've delved deeply into the art of garden and landscape design and eventually simplified the process for hundreds of townhouse owners who come to my townhouse gardening classes.

One of the great advantages and joys of owning a small garden comes from the fact that construction and planting of the garden can be finished faster than on a larger site. The end-result is also cheaper. Having less space to fill, you may be able to splurge occasionally on costlier materials that have more impact in a small garden. Also, smaller gardens mean less overall maintenance. If you truly love to putter around plants, you'll be able to have more finicky plants in a small space and the time to tend them well. You may also be able to accommodate a few important things you long for such as a small-scale water garden or a colorful flower border.

Contrary to popular belief, the process of creating beautiful outdoor spaces doesn't begin by buying a lot of plants and rushing out, shovel in hand, to "green up the place". In truly spectacular small gardens, the plants come after the needs of the gardens' inhabitants are first considered. This planning virtually guarantees that space will be available for relaxation and entertainment, the reasons most of us wish for a garden to begin with. Plants, of course are very important and they find their way to the design process as well—as a means to soften and enhance architectural features, as tools to create privacy, as things of beauty and as a means to make a very important connection with nature.

At the very beginning it's important to begin with a design or plan. Mostly it is a plan conceived and put on paper; sometimes it is a meticulous picture in the gardener's head; but good planning is essential to the creation of a well balanced, colorful and lovely garden. This is the step that most new gardeners often skip, yet how the garden is laid out, how materials are presented and how plants play off one another are all considerations in creating useful garden spaces. It's not just a matter of planting plants. It is instead a matter of manipulating the space to suit its inhabitants and in choosing plants that complement the design. Planning comes first. Planting is just the icing on the cake.

Many begin so enthusiastically. In their zeal to buy plants they completely overlook the design process. Others get discouraged by the simple rectangle of grass in their backyards which never becomes more than a highly mortgaged place for the garbage can and recycling bins. Some feel that there really isn't much they can do to liven up the space because they are renting. To all I say: take heart. With proper planning and attention to a few design principles, the space can become quite special and actually increase in value.

Re-sale value is an important consideration. For many people, the townhouse is merely a financial stepping stone towards a larger house somewhere down the line. These "transitory" homeowners want an affordable, beautiful landscape in a short period of time that will convey nicely when the house is sold. Other townhouse dwellers may be coping with someone else's gardening mistakes—seeking to correct them before they move on. Or they may be renting and prefer a nice garden for a season or two without spending a fortune.

Making a useful garden in a small space begins with careful assessment of one's priorities for the site. Some wish for a private, personal oasis of green in a very public world. Others seek to extend the indoor living areas of their homes for entertaining and relaxation without a lot of maintenance chores. Still others may want a space for the children to play or a spot to cultivate herbs, vegetables or lovely flowers. This book is for all of them.

Here, well thought-out designs for townhouse gardens are presented from a wide range of designers, landscape architects and garden professionals. These plans offer many inspiring design possibilities that don't require intense horticultural research or enormous outlays of cash. The book includes basic lessons in groundwork, soil preparation and garden maintenance. And for those who wish to do their own designing, all the basics of garden design are covered as well.

Because most townhouse gardens appear so limited and small, chapter three includes illusions and tricks designers use to bring atmosphere to small spaces. Chapter six focuses on combining plants effectively and includes lists of trees, shrubs, perennials, groundcovers and other plants particularly suitable for townhouse gardens in the northeastern part of the country. If you are gardening outside this area, you can still use the landscape plans, but be sure to consult a local nursery for plants that grow well in your area.

Here every aspect of townhouse gardening is covered to increase the enjoyment of your land and maximize the investment you have in your home. You'll be guided through top-quality designs with the easiest and best methods for turning your "blank canvas" of a yard into the townhouse garden of your dreams. Happy Gardening!

1.
Planning the Garden

*T*he typical gardens of yesteryear were huge by comparison to the stamp-sized yards we live in today. Unbelievably, it wasn't uncommon for a half-acre parcel to be considered a "small lot" in our grandmother's day. Houses, of course, were bigger too. Today, most of us have limited living space and even more limited outdoor space. Every inch counts and outdoor space has become more important than ever before. This is not only true for economic reasons, it is true because of what gardens can actually do for us. A tiny green space that we can nurture as our own becomes a sanctuary away from the "asphalt jungle".

A beautiful garden not only provides a place to nurture plants and ourselves, it visually expands the living area of the house and offers additional living space—an important consideration in homes large and small. Well chosen landscape features such as plants and patio materials also provide the opportunity to get out there and live in the "outdoor room" you pay so much for in your monthly mortgage payments. Though surrounded by other townhouses, outdoor rooms can be cozy, intimate, private and highly livable areas.

So how do you begin to create your townhouse sanctuary? The importance of a landscape plan or garden design cannot be stressed enough. At the very least, some kind of order will prevent the garden from descending into utter chaos and will help realize the potential of the space. Most garden experts approach the design of outdoor space the same way. Whether it's 100 square feet or 100 acres, they usually follow a four-part process. First they assess the needs of the client and find a style to work with. They then follow with a survey of the site. Third, they ponder over the possibilities of the project. They apply design principles, and may make many rough sketches before finally drawing landscape and planting plans.

You must decide what it is you want and settle on some sort of style, even if it is only a general idea of formal or informal. The first few decisions are the most important, for no matter how grand the garden is, if it does not please its owner it is not right. The first step begins with you. In the beginning, what is necessary is a little soul searching on your part before you dig the first hole or buy that first garden bench. You must know where you want to go before you begin your journey. So begin by asking, "What is my passion for the space?"

Garden Thoughts, Longings, Wishes and Desires

With me it was a need to create a blissful little "nest" during those first heady days of a new marriage. For you it will probably be something completely different. You have to ask yourself what a garden means to you. This is an important first-step because your answers and observations will become the core of every design decision you make for the garden.

Do you want a flower covered cottage? What flowers do you love the most? Is there a fragrance you remember from childhood? Is there water or rock or a glorious old gazebo in the gardens of your past? Are there flower colors you like or don't like? What atmosphere do you prefer, warm or sunny? Do you favor contemporary or formal decor in your house? In your travels did you fall in love with the quiet ancient gardens of Japan, or the dazzling exuberance of fountains and marble sculpture in Paris? Often the first clue to how the garden will evolve comes from what furnishings you decorate the interior of your house with. And while we're at it, take a good look at the facade of the house itself. Is it a dark contemporary box nestled in clusters of other townhouses in the woods, or a bricked colonial in a new subdivision of a thousand other townhouses with no canopy of trees?

Of course you won't be able to recreate the huge marble fountains of Rome in your tiny backyard, but knowing that you love them will enable you to incorporate their "flavor" somewhere in your design. Perhaps a piece of Mediterranean artwork can be nestled into the greenery and evoke the flavor of what you loved so much about Italy. This gives the garden your personal "stamp" which is what the art of designing a garden is all about.

In the beginning, you'll seek out your personal style. Take the time to fill out the garden planning worksheet on pages 13 and 14. Some people are very "garden specific". They hate the color yellow or eschew any particular fragrance in their gardens. Some hate thorns, others dislike a particular plant. I developed this valuable planning tool for students who come to my classes to assist them in determining their needs for their gardens.

In addition to the worksheet here, you might gather ideas from books, magazines, public gardens, flower and garden shows, garden tours and by looking at other neighborhood gardens. Clip pictures to save in a file and note everything that pleases you—from the teak bench you saw at the mall, to the lovely weeping tree at the flower show.

Finding Your Style—Informal or Formal?

If you go through all the information you're bound to accumulate from this exercise, you'll begin to see certain patterns emerging. When flipping through magazines and books, pay careful attention to exactly what it is about a scene that catches your eye. Is it the charming way the paving is laid, with plants allowed to fill in crevices and pockets in the stonework? Or is it the elegance of glossy boxwood borders repeated in a very geometric design? Pay careful attention to these details. They will signal your preference for formality or informality in the design you will create for your garden.

Typically informal gardens are asymmetrical affairs often full of blowzy, overgrown plants. The cottage gardens I so longed for early in my gardening career were informal. Natural waterfalls and ponds, wildlife gardens for birds and butterflies, flower borders, theme inspired gardens such as rock or fragrance gardens and gardens of Oriental influence are usually laid out informally. These are often very naturalized places dominated by large drifts of plants. The design normally involves gentle curves and sweeps in the lines of beds and borders, with straight lines occurring rarely, if ever.

Formal gardens, on the other hand, are usually laid out methodically in symmetrical geometric patterns. Plants are usually not allowed to grow out of bounds and are often bordered by strict enclosures of stone or hedging. In the eastern portion of the United States, boxwood is often the first choice for hedging formal gardens due to its glossy good looks and ability to accept frequent shearing. In formal gardens straight lines rule the day and meticulously groomed, tailored plantings dominate. Traditional herb gardens, "knot" gardens, Colonial gardens (think Mount Vernon), those Roman "water works" and maze gardens of Victorian England are examples of formality in garden design.

Deciding whether you are a "formal" garden person or an "informal" garden person is important. If you were decorating the living room of your home, you wouldn't grab any couch off the showroom floor and take it home, would you? Gardening is a lot like decorating. Once you've decided on the style you like, you begin to assess what the room actually needs. Perhaps you are a "formal" type. You like the green velvet wing back chairs at the furniture store. You've measured the room and decide that you could use two of the chairs with a lovely polished mahogany table between to set off the three cherry bookcases along the wall at the end of the room. Gardening is no different. You begin by finding a style and assessing your needs. You like the formal style of the green velvet chairs and assess that you need two chairs, not a dozen.

What You Want vs. What You Can Have

Okay, so you've filled out the garden planning worksheet and delved into your past to find out what a garden means to you. You've probed, you've discovered, you've fantasized. You've achieved a sense of enlightenment and know (or at least have a vague idea of) the type of garden you'd be most comfortable with. One hopes you don't discover a secret desire to recreate Versailles in your 200 square-foot backyard. I say this because occasionally new townhouse owners approach me with such grandiose ideas. They want huge labor-intensive English perennial borders, or entire meadows of grasses and native plants, or Dutch canals full of Japanese koi, or gigantic water spas for a dozen people...the list is endless. They want it all with the caveat that it must be continually flattering, full of something interesting to look at 365 days a year, maintenance-free, instantly private, spacious and completely obtainable for well under a few hundred dollars.

Sites vary enormously, but unless your townhouse comes with a backyard the size of Montana, you're not going to have it all. Believe me, you really don't want it all either. Over and over I end up chanting my mantra to these students: "Practice discretion, practice restraint." Keep it simple.

Narrow your list of priorities to a couple of things you desire from the garden. Perhaps it's to cultivate colorful, fragrant flowers for arranging in the house, or maybe it's to grow vegetables and herbs for gourmet cooking. It could be a desire for an area to entertain outdoors or a need for privacy—that often missing component in townhouse gardens. Over the years, the three most common prerequisites of my students have been a desire for privacy, a need for a hard surface for relaxation and entertainment and the wish for beautiful plants that are easy to maintain and interesting to look at throughout the year.

At this point if you decide to go no further in the process and hire the job out to a nursery or other garden professional, you'll at least be armed with the most valuable information the designer needs from you—your style and preferences for the site.

Garden Planning Worksheet

Name and Age of Each Family Member : _____

_____

_____

Pets: _____

Hobbies of Each Family Member: _____

_____

_____

What decor/garden style do you like? _____Formal?   _____ Informal?

Other Style (oriental, English cottage, modern, etc.) _____

What colors do you like? _____

Are there any plants or colors you dislike? _____

_____

Your Requirements:

_____ Entertaining Area   _____ Sunning Area

_____ Eating Area   _____ Pet Area

_____ Play Area   _____ Vegetable Garden

_____ Tree/Shade   _____ Service/Utility Area

_____ Trash Storage   _____ Compost/Potting Area

_____ Privacy/Screening   _____ Firewood Storage

_____ Lawn Area   _____ Other: _____

Features You Desire:

_____ Deck   _____ Gazebo

_____ Patio   _____ Hammock

_____ Outdoor Cooking Area   _____ Storage Shed   *Continued* _____

_____ Dog Run   _____ Water Garden

_____ Pool or Spa   _____ Greenhouse

_____ Night Lighting   _____ Irrigation System

_____ Statues or Sculpture   _____ Furniture

_____ Other: _____

Themes You Like: (fragrance, water, herbs, butterflies, color, etc_____
_____

Desired Effect of the Property:

_____ Flowers   _____ Foliage

_____ Seasonal Interest   _____ Low Maintenance

_____ Wildlife Benefit   _____ Other:
_____

"Hard" Landscape Materials You Like:

_____ Brick   _____ Gravel

_____ Flagstone   _____ European Cobbles

_____ Plain Concrete   _____ Stamped Concrete

_____ Wood Decking   _____ Aggregate

Existing Problems of the Site: (bad views, lack of privacy, drainage, lack of shade/sun, walkways too narrow ,etc._____
_____

Positive Features of the Site: (nice views, desirable plants, etc.) _____
_____

Budget for Project Costs: _____

Budget for Annual Landscape Maintenance:_____

_____ Flagstone   _____ European Cobbles

_____ Plain Concrete   _____ Stamped Concrete

Who the Experts Are and How They Can Help

Design is the subject on which most garden lovers get hung up. Not all of us possess the horticultural knowledge and design acumen of landscape architects and designers. In a small space, because every design decision is crucial and mistakes are so visible, it may pay to seek out the services of a professional. This is particularly true if you are overwhelmed by every plant you see and feel (as I often do) that the world will simply stop if you don't have one of everything in your tiny townhouse garden. Landscape designers have an uncanny ability to reign in those of us who want a beautiful, low-maintenance garden, but are themselves afflicted with the all too common "collector syndrome".

Consulting a professional is advisable if you are dealing with major liabilities such as an entire landscape renovation, an extremely steep slope or water problems. If you're faced with any of these kinds of issues consult an expert to assist you before construction of the garden begins.

The nomenclature of landscape professionals warrants explanation here because what they do, what they charge and the services they offer are so different. Landscape and garden designers are usually employees of nurseries who sell plants and install garden features like stone walls, patios, arbors and the like. Often their design fee is nominal and may be applied against the cost of the total landscape job. Usually, these professionals are avid gardeners themselves and are quite skilled at suggesting the best plants for your area. For this they are an invaluable resource. They should also be helpful in outlining the best materials for your patio and entertaining areas. Because features like patios, walls, fences and other major "hardscapes" are the most expensive elements of the overall design, you need to be very up-front about your budget to aid them in material selection.

Landscape architects are well-schooled, licensed professionals who are skilled in manipulating land. Their expertise is usually not needed for the design of smaller gardens unless, as mentioned above, there are major issues of terracing, regrading or water problems at hand. These professionals typically charge an hourly fee for consultations and another flat fee for drawn plans. Landscape architects, too, are often employed by nurseries, but may also be part of larger firms that specialize in commercial land planning.

Working With a Contractor

Frequently, the firm that designs your garden will be the firm that installs it. Or, if you've got a design you like and need the landscape installed, you'll work with a local nursery or landscape contractor to do the job.

One of the glories of creating a garden is the fact that so much of it can by done without the aid of hired contractors. If you are willing and able, you'll save a great sum by doing some or all of the work yourself. The process can become agonizing if you get in over your head though. Some of us may be skilled at carpentry, but how many of us actually have the time or resources to build a house? Building a garden is the same. The harder aspects, like building a patio or installing a brick wall, may be better left to the services of a professional. Even soil enrichment and the planting of heavy trees and shrubs may be too much work for some busy townhouse owners. Professional contractors can have an entire job installed in a much shorter period of time and they usually guarantee plants for six months or a year—two very good reasons to work with the pros.

To avoid trouble later, be very specific about your requirements when working with a contractor. Work from a well labeled plan that you have approved to be sure that all the elements you desire are included in the job, and put everything in writing to be sure that you are getting exactly what you want. Include pictures of materials if necessary. It pays to be clear about the company policy on plant guarantees as well. It isn't unusual to lose a few plants in a new landscape installation, and you'll want to be sure that these are replaced with identical plants in a timely fashion.

Establishing legal liability is important. Make sure that the contractor and any subcontractors on your property have adequate insurance. Always ask for and check references before making a deposit or signing a contract. You might also take the time to call the Better Business Bureau or small claims court in your town and ask if they have a file or outstanding cases against the company in question. Subcontractors should be reputable and responsible as well. Be sure to investigate every company that works on your job.

For a smooth relationship with your contractor agree on start and completion dates in advance. Be lenient enough to note that landscape contractors are at the mercy of the seasons and weather. Bad weather, however, should not be an excuse for a contractor to leave your project to finish another or take months on a job that should have taken a week.

The Rental Scenario

Perhaps you are renting your townhouse and wish for a lovely garden but don't want to spend a fortune on expensive plants and features that you won't be able to take with you. Often if a landlord knows that you are willing to do the work and can be shown the design on a well drawn plan, he will foot the bill for materials and plants or take a portion off the rent. After all, it's his investment you are enhancing and improving. My one regret is that the element you are apt to work hardest at—the soil—will not go with you when you move. Remember that many perennials can be divided and later moved to another house—leaving the landlord with plants and furnishing the beginnings of another garden as well.

If the landlord is not financially willing, stick with those features that you can enjoy in a relatively short period of time and choose things that you can take with you when you go such as decorative containers, trellises, artwork and furniture. Consider planting a garden of only annual plants— those plants that flower and die after only one season. A few companies offer all-annual wildflower seed mixes of beautiful flowers that will grow in prepared soil for one season. These mixes are ideal for covering ground quickly and are very low in cost. For instant impact in small spaces, consider softening walls and fences with inexpensive vine covered trellises. Annual climbers like morning glories, scarlet runner beans and hyacinth beans are easy to grow and do a great job of clothing vertical structures in the summer.

Vegetable or herb gardens can fill the need to garden in rented space and provide a culinary pay-back as well. Small gardens lend themselves beautifully to rows of edible plants such as tomatoes, carrots, squash, eggplant and peppers. What's more, if you prepare planting beds and decide to move, just lay a few strips of sod over the bare beds and water them well for a few weeks before your departure. The yard will be no worse for it.

Instead of spending money on expensive plants, you might rather splurge on beautiful outdoor furniture and buy decorative pots that can be planted and taken to a new home later. Beautiful garden arbors are now available that can be knocked down for travel to a new home and artwork like sculpture and wall-mounted garden fountains can always move when you do.

The Site Survey

Grab a pad of paper and go outside to take a good look around the place. Begin by making a rough sketch of the yard and take careful notes on its assets and liabilities. At this stage, you've got some ideas about what you'd like to see in the garden some day and now you must consider the site.

Outside, you may find that you desperately need screening for the ugly, belching air conditioning unit, or screening from the ugly, belching neighbors for that matter. Perhaps the garden sits in the baking sun all day and badly needs a source of shade. Are there overhead trees casting deep shade or is the shade more open and dappled? Note existing features that cannot be ignored like sidewalks, buildings, cars in the parking lot, ugly electrical boxes and neighboring structures. Is there no privacy or shelter? Is your front walkway too narrow? Is the concrete slab in the backyard ugly? Are existing shrubs large and over grown? Is there too much grass to maintain? Think of privacy, storage and access—access to the alley between townhouses, access to firewood or the water spigot. These are the garden's necessaries—the little realities that you will eventually marry harmoniously with your garden fantasies to create the garden of your dreams or, as in most marriages, grudgingly compromise into a place that you love despite its foibles.

Next, walk back inside and look out every window of the house to assess the view. Do you want to see a lovely garden when you look out your home office or kitchen window? If you're dealing with the prior owners' plants, take the time to identify them and remember that different things bloom at different times of the year so you may have to wait a season or two to identify all the bulbs and plants.

Assets are easier to note. Is there a stunning view you want to preserve? Perhaps there's a feature such as a neighbor's tree that can be "borrowed" into the design. You can actually landscape to make it appear as though the tree is a part of your own lot. This Oriental technique, called "borrowing the view", is frequently used in designing small spaces. Other assets might include beautiful patio paving built by previous owners or unique architecture like a spiral staircase. Any feature you wish to highlight should be noted on your rough drawing.

Measuring and Making A Scaled Drawing

After you have done the site survey, you'll be ready to make a detailed drawing of your yard. This is the design procedure that most new gardeners are apt to skip, but, as we've seen, it is the single most important step in making the garden. Measuring the space is important because your eyes can deceive you. What appears to you as a perfectly square piece of property while standing in your yard, may in fact be closer to a wedge shape or trian-

Scruffy, Unattractive Grass

View to Neighboring Townhouses - Need Privacy

Shade After 4 PM in Summer

Need Access to Service Area

Existing Patio Too Small

Kitchen   *Family Room*

E / N — S / W

Living Room

Sun All Day

Hard to Mow

Walkway Too Narrow

View to Parking Area

Busy Street Noise

Take notes on the assets and liabilities of the site to aid you in the design process later.

gle after you've finished measuring. Measure all major points such as walkways, entry doors, windows, utility boxes and existing plants. If you've recently gone to settlement on your townhouse, you may find a plat of the land in the settlement papers. In most cases, copies of this valuable document can be used to outline your garden on a scaled piece of paper.

When drawing the outlines of your property, begin with a sheet of $^1/_4$-inch grid paper. After measuring, you should be able to draw a pretty close approximation of your garden. Scale is important here. If the paper cannot accommodate one square equal to one foot of actual space, use a scale of one square equaling two or five feet until you get the plan to fit onto the paper. I often tape two sheets of paper together to make the design fit in a scale of one square equaling one foot because working with a larger drawing is less complicated and the drawing can accommodate more garden features without looking cluttered on paper.

Once the basic outline of your property is on paper, make about a dozen copies so that you can "play" with the garden on paper. With the first sheet, incorporate the "site notes" from your site survey. Use arrows to point out changes in grade and any nice vistas or views you want to preserve. Also mark the location of existing plants you may want to keep. Finally, mark where North appears to aid you in selecting plants suitable to the site later. This first drawing will be your official "site survey" and assist you when you go on to create the design for your garden.

TOWNHOUSE TIP

No landscape is maintenance-free, but you can reduce maintenance to a minimum by combining hard features such as stone paving with shrubs, small trees and a groundcover such as pachysandra, ajuga or periwinkle to keep weeds down. Consider good quality paving instead of a lawn and use evergreen shrubs of colored and variegated foliage for visual interest. For further interest, grow seasonal flowers in containers and replace them regulary for colorful displays throughout the years.

2.
Elements
of
Good Design

*I*n Chapter One you assessed your needs and surveyed the site. By now, you've drawn a scaled drawing of your property and have several copies of your drawing to work with. From these blank copies, creative design ideas will flow and you will eventually draw a garden plan. In the beginning, you shouldn't be concerned with placing specific plants on the drawing. The selection of specific plants comes later when a "planting plan" is created. For now be concerned with the shape of the space and how it evolves into a design capable of handling the needs you have. You'll concentrate on laying out "hard" areas such as pathways, a deck or patio area and follow by deciding in a general way where the best place for plants would be.

Many of us would be ill-tempted to build a house or manufacture a car without a set of blueprints. It's the same with a landscape. A good plan saves time and money in the long run by giving you a more accurate picture of the work ahead. Even if you cannot afford to install the entire landscape immediately, a good plan will help you select priority areas and help assess where you'd like to spend your money in the first and subsequent years.

Now, it's not imperative that you know where every last tulip bulb is to go, but having an idea of where large items like the patio and the path to the rear alley would best be laid out makes subsequent decisions easier. When it does come time to select plants, you'll have assessed the site thoroughly and will know what the soil and sun conditions are so that you can select the right plants for the right places.

The Shape of Your Garden

To begin, assess the overall shape of your garden space as it appears on paper. Is it a square, rectangle or L-shaped space? Square gardens often need a sense of movement to avoid the feeling of tight enclosure. Shapes such as circles, ovals, rectangles, octagons, squares, grids and free-flowing curves all play a part in shaping small spaces. Landscape designers typically design in one of three "shape themes" based on circles, diagonals or grid patterns. From the use of these simple shapes a garden is born.

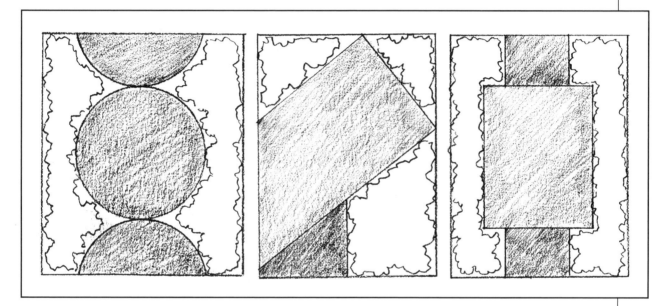

Circular designs are one of the most beautiful and useful themes for breaking up the monotony of a rectangular garden, while diagonal designs create a strong sense of movement. Small garden spaces are often designed on the diagonal—across the longest lines the space has to offer. By pivoting garden features on the diagonal you'll exploit the maximum potential of the space and make a more spacious visual presentation. Visual movement then flows diagonally taking advantage of the widest length of the space. It gives a feeling of openness that would not exist if the space were planned in a more formal geometric pattern.

Squares or "grids" are commonly used in formal designs where garden beds are geometrically laid out. This is well suited to long narrow gardens where individual "rooms" can be created by dividing the long narrow space into more manageable areas, connected by a common path between them.

Examples of circular, diagonal and grid themed gardens.

Gardens built within a square yard require some form of "movement" to alleviate the closed in feeling. If a diagonal design is not possible, a focal point can be located at the far edge of the garden to draw the eye forward and through the main axis of the garden. "Axis" refers to a real or imaginary line around which the parts of the garden are arranged. In a small space the main axis might run from the back door through the patio area to a decorative piece of statuary at the end of the garden. This acts as a visual invitation to explore the space. Often, this inward focus is chosen when there is no view from the garden. With no view, you must create one and the focal point is placed within the tranquil setting of the garden.

Structures also create interest. Built-in raised beds are interesting not only because of their shapes, but because they lend height to the design. Large, built-in beds are often the ideal solution for soggy or infertile areas and prevent a lot of the bending and stretching that goes along with a ground level garden. Their bulk also aids in creating structure in small gardens and their edges can provide additional seating areas as well.

The first tenet in laying out the patterns and shapes of your garden is to keep it simple. Nothing is as beautiful as a perfect circle of grass in a rectangular space, bordered perhaps by brick or cobble and planted heavily to obscure the boundaries. What a picture of simplicity it is on paper and how easy to maintain compared to a lot of squiggles and nonsensical curves! Larger shapes really are better to define space and one broad curve is eminently better than a lot of short stops and starts in tiny spaces. The depth of beds and borders is important too. Some owners of small townhouse yards think too small for their site. Don't be afraid to bring borders well away from the permanent architectural structures and make them deep. The deeper, the better. A deep bed, six or more feet away from the fence or walls of the house allows for a mixed border of small trees, shrubs and other decorative plants which is eminently more interesting than a narrow line of hedging.

Consider these guidelines as you take blank copies of the site drawing and sketch shapes within the space. Some gardeners even cut out circles, squares and triangles from construction paper to experiment with until they find a pleasing design. These shapes can represent anything—a patio, a group of plants, a water feature—whatever pleases you and fits well into the space. You may want to make three separate drawings using the three themes of circle, diagonal and grid as the basis of each. Drawing a design three ways will give you a clear idea of the many ways the garden can evolve.

The Principles of Design

The art of designing space is complex, but not beyond the grasp of most committed garden lovers. Like painting, sculpting and many of the other arts, garden design relies on certain principles which, when understood, will help guide you in transforming your lot.

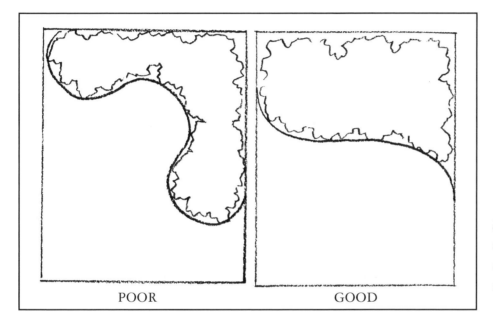

POOR   GOOD

Sweeping curves are far better than a lot of squiggles.

Mass and Void

You could just pave the yard over and be done with it, but a solid sheet of concrete won't provide the cozy ambiance that a well thought out patio and plantings will. What that solid yard of concrete lacks, among other things, is the mass of plants around it to give balance to the site. "Mass" is the term designers use to define structure and plantings in the garden and "void" is the open area between them. In truly beautiful gardens there is a gentle balance between mass and void. You must not design too large a patio for it may be out of balance with the rest of the site, and conversely don't overplant the yard and fill up all the open spaces. It's imperative to strive for balance.

Scale and Proportion

Two other design terms also fit right into this frame of thinking—scale and proportion. "Scale" is the visual weight that things carry within the garden. You wouldn't cram a ten-foot sofa into a ten-foot room, would you? In the garden, it's best not to install structures and plants that will eventually overwhelm the space. Many gardeners are guilty of this gardening "faux pas"—designing decks far larger than the site can comfortably carry, or purchasing plants that will eventually grow way out of scale to the site. Don't go overboard with a lot of small things either. Most new gardeners think in terms that are less than bold for small spaces, but boldness is often just what the garden needs to make it splendid. The design may evolve around one well placed feature like a beautiful tree or interesting paving.

All the features of your garden should be in the correct scale or proportion to surrounding buildings and garden features. "Proportion" is the visual balance of the garden. All the features must be in a balanced relationship to each other and all the features must sit well within the site. Just as you should not place all your furniture on one side of a room, you will not place all the garden's features on one side of the garden. Features such as paths, patios, water gardens, plantings and overhead structures should be balanced throughout the site. Play with structures and plants on paper, continually adding or editing them until a well balanced garden is achieved.

When including the things you want on your drawing, make sure they keep within the balance of mass and void and do not throw the space out of proportion by being too large or too small. Every structure should add something to the whole, and every open space should balance with the masses around it. There shouldn't be too much structure and there shouldn't be too much open space either. Other design principles come into play in the creation of beautiful garden space as well. A few of the most important ones follow:

Unity—Unity is achieved when all the parts of the garden form a pleasing whole and all the elements are working together. The most notable example of unity is Giverney—Monet's garden outside Paris, where every structure throughout the garden is painted the same shimmering hue of blue-green. Furniture, containers, bridges, arbors and even the shutters on the house are all unified by the same color and contribute to the garden design throughout the seasons. You don't have to paint every feature the same color, but you may choose to unify certain aspects of your design. Perhaps all your containers could be of one material like terra cotta or all the furniture and gates comprised of black iron.

Simplicity—Keep the design simple and the garden will be beautiful. The smaller the garden, the simpler the design of its space should be.

Variety—Variety is the spice of life and in the garden enough variety should be apparent without overwhelming with clutter. Choose accents carefully, keeping one interesting focal point in any given "view" of the garden. Like a movie director, use your hands to frame each side of the garden to be sure that too many accents do not exist.

Focal Points—Every garden should have at least one focal point—an artificial or natural point of visual interest. The eyes come to rest on objects or special plants because they are different. Here it's quality, not quantity, that counts. Gardeners should not go overboard busying up the scenery with knick-knacks. One substantial feature, accented by lovely plantings, always looks better than dozens of tiny artifacts strewn about.

Balance—Balance relates to equality between the masses and voids in the garden. The visual weight of all the garden's elements should be presented as a balanced whole throughout the space, just as you would place furniture around a room, not all at one end.

Color—Color can make a garden feel more or less expansive. It can open up space or create a cozy, intimate feeling. Generally, cooler colors like blue, white and pale pastel tones are more expansive while warmer colors like red, orange and acid yellow make space feel more closed in. This is not to say that hot colors like scarlet and orange aren't welcome in the small garden. Jolts of hot color are often just what pale plantings need to show them off at their best. A few red tulips interspersed in a sea of blue forget-me-nots are a memorable sight, as are scarlet wands of red-hot poker against a backdrop of violet butterfly bush. No matter what colors you love, it's wise to stick to a palette of no more than two or three colors in any garden.

Structure—In the best gardens there is an underlying structure to the plantings. Often a magnificent old stone wall or dark green hedge provides a backdrop that shows flower colors at their best. Provide structure for colorful plantings in your garden with fences, raised beds and hedges of dark evergreens like yew, boxwood, holly, laurel or arborvitae.

Texture—Gardens are not made by flowers alone. In fact, it's often the foliage you're left with for the greater part of the year, so be sure to choose plants that look pleasing together when not in bloom. Many gardeners strive for a carefully "layered" look in their gardens. This works especially well in shade gardens where one leaf form plays off another. Group slender leaf forms with rounded plant forms and provide accents with spiked foliage throughout plantings.

Use spiked foliage as an attention-grabber in the garden.

Laying Out the Garden on Paper

As you progress in shaping the space you will eventually determine the shapes that are the most pleasing to you. It's important to remember that the paper you are working on is only one dimension of a multi dimensional space. Your garden will have many vertical spaces like fence and house walls to deal with. Other structures like container gardens, raised beds, sunken pools and furniture will jump off the page into real life as the garden is created. It's important to keep these three dimensional elements in mind when planning. Take time to visualize these features as they will appear in the garden.

A camera is a helpful tool at this stage. Often designers shoot pictures of the empty garden, then place overlays of tracing paper on the pictures, drawing on new elements to test them out on the site. This is much easier than trying to visualize the entire landscape in your mind and may help you form stronger ideas about what will work and what will not work in your garden. A scaled drawing should never be abandoned, however, because structural elements such as seating areas should be plotted out exactly on your plan to allow room enough for moving freely around the garden.

Lawn and Turf Areas

Should a lawn be a part of your townhouse garden? As an instructor, I am often asked this question. The answer depends on a lot of variables, the first of which is the individuality of the space. Because the area is small to begin with, the ground will be under constant foot-traffic and grass is not the most practical choice of "flooring" in terms of wearability and cleanliness—not to mention the question it raises of where to put the mower. A paved surface offers many more options for furniture placement and ease of maintenance. Why struggle with patchy grass, mowers and legions of weeds when a beautiful patio may bring you more joy?

If it's the ground-covering effect of green grass you want, perhaps a grass substitute would be better. In areas where the look of a lawn is desired, but the lawn will not actually be tread upon, low, creeping plants may be used such as thyme, moss, clover, liriope, ajuga or creeping phlox.

If you have an end-unit townhouse or an unusually large lot, you may wish to pave a portion of the garden for entertaining and have a small area of green grass. Strive to keep the shape of the lawn simple to make maintenance easier. Plan for multiples of your mower width and edge the area with a mowing strip of pavers or bricks to keep grass from encroaching upon beds and borders. To prevent a lot of stops and starts later, plan curves according to the turning radius of your mower.

For a lush lawn, choose the proper grass seed for your region and site needs. Reputable nurseries will have the best seed for sun or shade and for high traffic areas. Finally, for a truly unique design treatment, consider installing the lawn on a different level. A lawn sunk down a step or raised up a step lends a point of interest to the design especially when surrounded by edges of stone or brick.

Creating Atmosphere

If you are without a splendid view, one of the best ways to make your space special is to turn the focus of the garden inward. If you're facing other townhouses or looking at a busy street, then obscure the property lines by placing a thick screen of plantings at the boundaries of the property in your design. This will give the impression of greater space. This also turns the garden focus inward and is one of the best design decisions you can make when the outward view is less than desirable.

Making the garden special is up to your own unique interpretation of the space. In gardening, like other art forms, there is room for individuality, even eccentricity. Fragrance plays a key role in establishing ambiance in some gardens as does the sound of water, the presence of butterflies, sculpture or even the plants themselves.

In gardening, as in any other art, the ultimate vision of perfection is in the eye of the beholder. Many gardeners make their environment special by the use of "themes" or specialties. It's worthwhile to explore different garden styles and themes that may be incorporated into your garden. Some of the unique gardens I've admired over the years are included in the following list of specialty gardens.

Species and Collectors' Gardens. These are collections of specific types of plants such as iris, roses, azaleas, hosta or rhododendrons. Collectors often hybridize and breed the plants they love. They become collectors after falling under the spell of one particular variety of plant.

Color Theme Gardens. Gardens can be planted in single colors for a stunning effect. The all-white garden at Sissinghurst Castle in England is perhaps the most famous and stunning example; although blue, pink, yellow or even variations on a green theme are seen as well. These types of gardens are often enlivened with careful placement of foliage plants to complement flowers. For example, grey lambs ears may be used in a garden of blue to accentuate the coolness of the flowers.

Wildlife Gardens. A garden can be made to attract birds, small mammals, hummingbirds, amphibians and butterflies. This is my favorite kind of garden because wildlife makes the gardening experience so much richer and real habitats are disappearing at an alarming rate. Water, a source of food and thick plantings that afford cover and protection will mimic habitat and attract creatures to most backyards.

Children's Gardens. Children love to nurture and grow things and a garden just for them can be a magical place to play and discover nature. Consider ideas like a "pizza garden" where tomatoes, basil, parsley and oregano are grown for making pizza. You may also create a secret "fort" under the shelter of a weeping tree, plant a patch of strawberries or a row of blueberry bushes or even grow a cottage garden at the door of a Victorian playhouse.

Colonial Gardens. This is a garden planted with flowers, herbs and other plants that might have been used in and around the house during colonial times for food, medicine, dye or spice. It's the perfect garden for Colonial-styled townhouses.

Water Gardens. Water is naturally calming and makes a wonderful addition to the garden environment. Fish and water lilies add a special ambiance to water gardens, as do bog gardens around the edge of the water.

Rock and Alpine Gardens. A group of miniature alpine plants tucked into the crevices of rocks or rock walls present unique charm to small gardens. Alpine gardening is perfect for containers like English or concrete troughs as well.

Moonlight Gardens. A garden can be designed in white, grey or luminous pastel colors to be viewed at night. The effect when combined with plants that emit heady fragrances is a subtle delight to the senses.

Many people, having gardened long enough, will fall in love with a style, specialty or theme in their gardens. Eventually you may find that you have a passion for herbs or that you can't live without a hundred daylilies in your townhouse garden. This passion is what gardening is all about. Often it's a matter of creating an atmosphere where there has been absolutely nothing before.

To create atmosphere with permanent structures you may consider building something substantial such as a pergola over a patio for instant impact. Train vines up and over the structure and you'll have a quick shortcut to a great garden as well as much needed privacy from overhead onlookers. In small spaces you must learn to combine function with ornament. Turn a simple tool shed into a charming potting shed rather than screening it from view. The trick to creating ambiance is to work with what you have.

Gardens situated in very shady, almost damp areas often seem most in need of ambiance. In these types of yards there are many ways of creating atmosphere. A thorough cleaning should reveal the virtues and liabilities of the area. Where darkness completely overwhelms, you may choose to paint the walls a light color to open up the space and clothe the walls with climbing plants. Vines such as climbing hydrangea soften the austerity of bare walls, while the use of light colored flowering plants like white impatiens, variegated ferns and cream colored caladiums will further brighten up the space. A few savvy gardeners install mirrors on walls to visually expand dark areas and increase the available light.

For nighttime atmosphere select grey or white flowering and foliage plants to shimmer under the sky. These pale colors seem almost luminescent in the darkness which creates another illusion apart from the daytime mood of the garden. Outdoor lighting, and candlelight too, are important parts of evening ambiance as well.

TOWNHOUSE TIP

For year-round interest in the garden choose evergreens and interplant them with plants chosen for their seasonal interest. For winter interest, the evergreen Foster holly can be combined with red-twig dogwoods which have scarlet stems. Or for summer interest, combine a hedge of evergreen yews with flowering perennial plants. The dark green of the yew highlights all flower colors beautifully.

3.
Magic in the Design

*F*or years British gardeners have used clever deceptions in pocket-sized gardens. With skillful design of space and the use of innovative materials they design tiny gardens that appear larger and more spacious than they really are. Savvy gardeners on this side of the Atlantic can take a lesson from the British by placing plants artfully to create mystery, spark interest, create intrigue and provide the garden with a sense of distance and depth. By changing levels, creating movement and using color the garden can be manipulated to make small spaces interesting. Most intriguing though is the use of illusions or visual deceptions. Like the magician that fools us into seeing what clearly isn't there, clever garden designers create distractions and illusions to maximize the potential of the smallest of spaces. Even the smallest garden can be helped in one or more of these ways. One just needs to understand these optical illusions in order to use them.

Creating Mystery

If you arrange your garden so that one part of it is hidden, you've instantly created curiosity in the mind of the visitor. A gentle, highly planted curve in the design invites exploration too. The garden seems more spacious because you're wondering what's around the bend in the yard. No matter if it's just the garden gate that leads to the alley; if you've concealed it, you've created a surprise and small surprises make small gardens interesting.

Even the shape of the lawn or patio can relay a sense of expansiveness in small gardens. In a rectangular or square garden you may opt for a circular lawn or patio. This is eminently more interesting than a stone or grassy square. Uninterrupted straight lines make the space seem smaller than it already is. The eye is drawn to the end of the garden too quickly. Use a sweeping curved path instead and create a sense of mystery. Large C- or S-shaped curves work best, so avoid wiggling, squiggling lines. The goal is to create a strong design statement and slow the eye down on its journey through the garden.

Creating Movement

Some gardens benefit from strong visual movement in the design itself. Paving, for instance, can be laid so it flows diagonally to direct attention to a focal point or specific place in the garden. Because diagonal lines are visually expansive, a square or rectangular patio will seem more spacious and exciting when paving units are laid diagonally, rather than grid-like. Diagonal lines are also a good way to invite exploration in L-shaped spaces when attention needs to be directed to the space around a corner or bend.

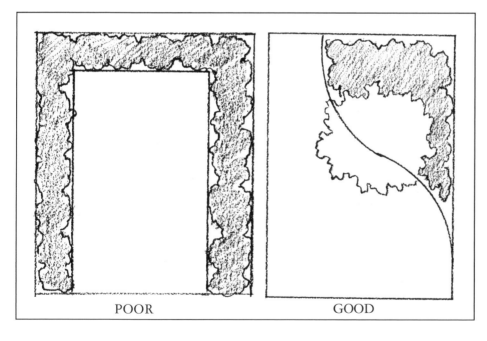

POOR   GOOD

A flowing, curved bed creates a feeling of spaciousness, movement and a sense of mystery. One wonders what is just around the corner.

Changing Levels

A change in level, be it a step up or down, is interesting. Many of the finest gardens contain a change in grade to make the space more intriguing. Even if the yard is entirely flat, a step up to a raised platform or patio creates a different aspect from which to view the garden. Be sure to make all steps highly visible for safety's sake though. An obvious transition, such as from the lawn to the first white, wooden step of a gazebo, is absolutely apparent and can prevent accidents.

Retaining a slope in a small garden can turn a liability into another terrific opportunity for creating interest. Small slopes are usually retained with stone or timber walls and can be heavily planted with draping foliage for interest. To do double duty in the garden, make these walls high enough to provide additional seating in the garden.

Major slopes eat up valuable space in townhouse gardens and can be quite a nuisance. If the garden is relatively level, but slopes away from the house, consider planting it with a groundcover and a "grove" of three or four small trees for privacy and low maintenance. If there is no level ground at all, some sort of leveling or regrading will be necessary and a retaining wall will have to be constructed. As I said earlier, this is not the type of job you should take on yourself if the slope is steep. The higher the retaining wall, the more complex the job. Consult a landscape architect to correct severe slope problems.

Creating Distance and Depth

Diminishing trellises create the illusion of depth in small spaces. You may add a painted mural or mirror at the center to further the illusion.

Visual perception of space can actually be altered in small gardens, creating the illusion of depth or length. Deep spaces always seem more spacious, but in spaces that lack depth, pathways can actually be constructed to narrow at the far end. This "long view" gives the perception of greater length. Add a piece of artwork at the end and you will have provided a point of visual interest. This creates the illusion that the pathway is longer than it actually is. Distance can also be visually altered by placing plants closer together as they recede in the distance.

Long, narrow gardens will appear wider if features are laid out on the diagonal. Visual movement then flows from side to side, taking advantage of the widest space in the garden. For a more formal approach, use interlocking circles of lawn or pathways to create interest and give the impression of greater depth.

Walls and fences can be altered with the use of trelliswork that actually exhibits diminishing proportions. The slats of the trellis are actually slanted inward to trick the eye into perceiving a depth that simply isn't there and is used in some of the most famous gardens in the world. To further the illusion you might use a mirror behind such trelliswork and plant the edges heavily.

Colors

Plant color can also be used to advantage in small gardens to create mystery and depth. Position airy shrubs and trees in front of dense hedges so that you see the background only through lacy foliage or twigs. This creates dimension and a sense of depth.

Flower colors should not be the only consideration when planning for color in the garden. The beauty of landscaping and choosing plants is that every plant comes in its own shade of green. Shades and tones of green foliage will advance or recede in the garden just as flower colors do. Dark blue-green hollies tend to recede into the distance, while their yellow-green cousins advance. Place light colored or variegated plants in front of darker green plants for maximum depth perception.

Look at the exterior of your townhouse. Is it warm red brick or cool grey clapboard? These warm or cool tones will not only dictate the color of paving material to use, they will dictate the warm or cool colors in the plants you buy. For example, by matching warm toned plants with a warm toned brick exterior and a warm toned paving, you'll coordinate the garden beautifully and easily.

The Element of Surprise

Creating areas that seem to be "just around the corner" are a way designers build depth and add excitement to mini-sized yards. A secret, unseen area will come as a pleasant surprise as the garden conceals and reveals itself.

In your garden you might also strive to create a small "folly" that garden visitors will delight in. This unseen or hidden "treat" might be a piece of sculpture hidden in the greenery, or a tiny fountain nestled deep in the plants surrounding the patio. These small discoveries will make your garden unique.

On larger sites latticework can be used to section off gardens and further create rooms within rooms. Latticework will effectively screen "service" areas without becoming as oppressive as solid wood walls. You might use a vine covered trellis wall to shield a service area for the trash can and potting bench. Some clever gardeners cut arches or decorative windows out of walls and trellises so they can glimpse the view beyond—

another way to expand the feeling of spaciousness. These framed vistas "borrow" scenery and immediately make the garden seem larger. You may even soften these windows to the outside world with hanging boxes or baskets brimming with plants to make the visual transition softer.

Garden "windows" can take many forms. Perhaps a small framed octagonal opening can be cut into the gate or a larger, shuttered window may be situated in a fence wall to capture a wonderful view. Arched openings may also be cut into walls of trellis under a deck to create a lighter atmosphere.

Creating Illusions

In the garden the use of clever tricks and illusions can make a person believe the space is actually larger than it is. Mirrors are reflective by nature and when strategically placed in the garden, they can open up space and create spacious "false perspectives" too. In archways, along walls, against gates or anywhere there is a desire to add extra dimension, you may hang a mirror. To make them believable in the garden, frame mirrors with plants or cover them with latticework.

Some gardeners begin by hanging a mirror on the fence or garden wall and softening its edges with plants. This trick immediately brings light into the darkest of gardens and visually expands the space as well. You could even mount a beautiful iron gate over the mirror to give the feeling of another room just beyond. Mirrors also work well to expand water features. A small rectangular water feature can be visually doubled in length by hanging a mirror behind it.

I have seen decorative murals painted on garden walls to give the impression that there's another garden just beyond the gate. This is an impressive and unique way to create a focal point in small gardens. For convincing results, the mural itself should appear to recede well into the distance. To make the illusion even more convincing, you might hinge a real door next to the scene that remains partially open. These garden highlights are ideal candidates for night lighting to bring more attention to them.

Screening and Distraction

Screening works to hide ugly features, but you can also create distractions to draw attention away from what is undesirable. Screen property boundaries with hedges or informal plantings to create privacy and produce an inward focus to the garden. If you screen the boundaries of your property, you might consider doubling the thickness of the hedging to create more visual depth. Varying the type of plants rather than using a solid hedge of one type lends depth and mystery too. Or try interplanting shrubs, vines, small trees and other plants so that they undulate along areas you wish to screen.

Artwork, a striking specimen plant or a lovely water feature works well at focusing attention on what is great about the garden instead of what is unattractive. Place the focal point well away from the feature you want to ignore. In the case of the air conditioning unit, you might conceal it behind a vine covered trellis, but you might also put a lovely wall fountain across the yard well away from the unit to call attention there.

Intrusions into townhouse gardens come from all sides, even from above when the neighbor's windows overlook you. For overlooking nuisances consider the shelter of trees. A canopy of trees is one of the best solutions to the problem of overhead intrusions and unattractive views beyond the walls of the garden. Small ornamental trees like redbuds, dogwoods, serviceberries and ornamental cherries create a shady bower to live under in the summer—safe from the intruding eyes of other townhouse dwellers. In the absence of trees, vine-covered pergolas or canopies may provide both shade and privacy.

TOWNHOUSE TIP

If you wish to help the garden along to maturity consider purchasing one or two mature trees or well established shrubs from the start. Combined with rich furnishings, overflowing container gardens and well constructed structures in the garden, these large-scale plants will help the garden look mature, even if it's in its infancy.

4.
Designs for Townhouse Gardens

*F*ifteen landscape designs suitable for a wide range of townhouse gardens are presented in this chapter. Each design includes a flat plan, a planting list, a description of the garden, plus a drawing of a section of the garden. You may choose to reproduce any of the designs in exact detail, so you won't go wrong, or create your own unique plan, drawing on these for inspiration. In most cases the designs can be installed by the average do-it-yourselfer in a season or two, but more ambitious work like laying patio pavers in mortar should probably be left to a professional.

Before you start, a word about homeowners associations is in order. Many townhouse developments have homeowners associations that are governed by strict rules and regulations. Often landscape improvements must be "approved" by the homeowners association or an architectural committee set up by the representatives of the association. Many homeowners are hesitant to make major changes to their bare lots, fearing the wrath and rules of the homeowners association. Beautiful gardens are an asset to the entire community and no one should be put off or afraid of these organizations. It's important to remember that the association exists to ensure that quality, high standards and value of the neighborhood are preserved.

Associations are more likely to approve of improvements that are clearly laid out and logically presented. In other words, show them the plan, lay out the garden on paper and draw a rendering if you can. Be as clear as you can about your intended use of the space. If you receive a rejection for a garden idea or structure, ask to appeal it. Most homeowner associations have an appeal process. You may be required to speak with your neighbors and obtain their consent before proceeding with your plans, or the board may loosen stringent community limitations for the benefit of all. In many cases, though, an appeal to the board that governs the association can result in a positive outcome. Most homeowners associations are concerned with preserving property values and excellent landscaping is one of the best ways to increase home value.

Beautiful garden designs are presented here, with detailed landscape plans and planting lists. The sizes of the yards are varied and you may find that the plan you like is too small, narrow or large for the space you have to work with. If your lot is too small to accommodate the plan you prefer you may adapt it by eliminating groups of plants and rearranging the space slightly. Usually all it takes is a little re-positioning of plants. On larger lots you may increase the size of the hardscape or lawn, make planting beds deeper or repeat groups of plants to fill the space. Make sure, however, that the proportion of the space isn't thrown off by your adjustments.

Plants too can be changed to accommodate color or variety preferences or climatic conditions. Here the planting lists are very specific, listing the common name followed by the botanical Latin name with the specific cultivar name in parentheses. A number appears in parentheses after the Latin name to indicated the quantity that should be purchased. The "botanical nomenclature" is very important to have on hand, not to impress your friends with, but to be sure you are buying the correct plants from the nursery. There are many types of spruce trees, for example, but only one or two would be suited to a tiny townhouse garden. The dwarf Alberta spruce, as you will see, is recommended on one of the plans. The common name, dwarf Alberta spruce, appears on the plant list and is followed by the botanical name in parentheses, (Picea glauca 'Conica'). To buy any ordinary spruce tree would be disastrous, because most spruces grow upward of 50 feet tall or more——a mistake for any townhouse garden.

The botanical name is given in Latin and appears in italics on the lists of plants. It is often followed by the cultivar name in singular quotes. The word "cultivar" is an abbreviation of the term, "cultivated variety". This individual and often unique name is especially important when choosing plants because plants can vary so much within their own species. Daylilies are a good example. There are literally thousands of named cultivars in existence. You may encounter names like 'Hyperion', 'Happy Returns' and 'Hello Dolly' in daylily catalogs and on plants tags in the nursery. These are the names the plant breeder gives the plant when it is first discovered, bred in quantity and put up for sale on the open market. The names become synonymous with that plant's color, fragrance and form—— hence, once a 'Hyperion' daylily, always a 'Hyperion' daylily. It is very important to pay special attention to the specific cultivar name to be sure you are getting exactly what you want. Occasionally you will encounter the abbreviation "spp." on plant lists, which means that some but not all of the species are appropriate. For example, you might see "Hosta spp." in parentheses following a listing for hosta. This means that many of the hosta varieties will be appropriate for that garden; a few, however may be too large or too small.

Each garden plan is labeled alphabetically to correspond with the plant lists. Occasionally a number appears in parentheses after a letter on the plan. This indicates the number of plants that should be planted in that location. In some instances a specific plant mentioned won't be available, or you may not like a plant listed. You may substitute a plant of another type or color, but be sure to select plants that reflect the flavor of the garden. Examine how the texture of one plant looks next to that of its neighbor and be sure you assess a plant's mature height and size will be before you buy. With careful thought and consideration you can achieve terrific results.

TOWNHOUSE TIP

Be sure to provide a suitable backdrop for the objects you display in the garden. Elevate a favorite piece on a pedestal or even on vine-covered stacks of bricks so that its importance is conveyed. When choosing art objects for the garden, remember that pale colored items show off best against dark backgrounds and dark objects show off best against lighter backgrounds.

The Designs

A Low-Maintenance Front Yard

Garden for Evening Entertainment

A Garden for Under a Deck

A Contemporary Garden

A Fragrant Side Yard Garden

A Garden for a Sloping Site

A Birdwatcher's Garden

A Garden for Hummingbirds and Butterflies

An End-Unit Front Yard

A Deck-Top Garden

A Tiny Townhouse Garden

A Shady Garden

The KinderGarden

A Low-Maintenence Back Yard

A Cottage Garden of Edibles

A Low-Maintenance Front Yard

Many people move to townhouses to get away from the chores a large yard demands. They prefer landscapes that enhance the house without all the hassles of annual replanting and the upkeep that some finicky plants require. This entry garden is suited to a shaded north aspect or to a site sheltered by nearby trees. The foundation bed incorporates a graceful arc that flows over the lawn, across the front walk, and terminates at the property line. Bricks line the narrow walkway, dressing up the plain concrete and adding valuable width. This border not only adds additional inches on each side of the walk, it draws attention to the entry of the house. The overall effect is enhanced by the permanent aspects like the bench placed next to the door, walkway materials and architecture that require little maintenance.

In sunnier areas you may use a tree that is more substantial like a sourwood *(Oxydendrum arboreum)* or flowering crabapple *(Malus spp.)*. The inkberry can take sun, but replace the rhododendron with a pyramidal-shaped dwarf alberta spruce *(Picea glauca* 'Conica'). Daylilies *(Hemerocallis hybrids)* may be used in place of shade loving hostas and the azaleas could be replaced with spiraea *(Spiraea x bumalda* 'Anthony Waterer').

A. Carolina Silverbell,
　　(Halesia carolina) (1)
　　　　Note: Select a multi-trunk
　　　　specimen.
B. Inkberry
　　(Ilex glabra 'Shamrock') (8)
C. Robin Hill Azalea
　　(Rhododendron 'Sir Robert') (4)
D. Dwarf Rhododendron
　　(Rhododendron yakusimanum) (1)
E. Variegated Host
　　(Hosta 'Francee') (9)
　　　　Note: Interplant daffodil
　　　　bulbs around hosta.
F. Periwinkle
　　(Vinca minor) (48)
G. Seasonal annuals in containers (2)

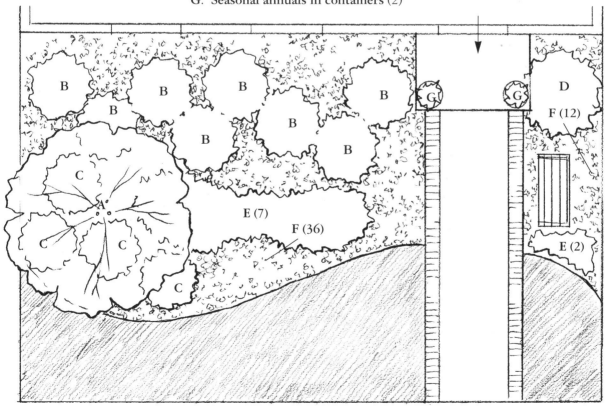

A Garden for Evening Entertainment

Designed with an emphasis on good looking architectural hardscapes, this garden presents a lovely view from the interior of the house and acts as an additional room for visitor "overflow" during parties. Here, a versatile brick patio is married with raised stone walls around a water garden and tree well at the center of the garden. The sound of trickling water attracts guests to the garden pool where the wall around the pool can double as extra seating. The fountain in the pool can also be lit with a spotlight to draw attention to it.

Trees and shrubs create the structure, while borders of seasonal plants are changed throughout the year. This makes it possible to create garden themes for any occasion. As a nighttime "stroll" garden for guests, the garden can be planted with white and grey colors that shimmer under the moonlit sky. Night lighting with strings of white "fairy" lights among the trees will also create a festive atmosphere.

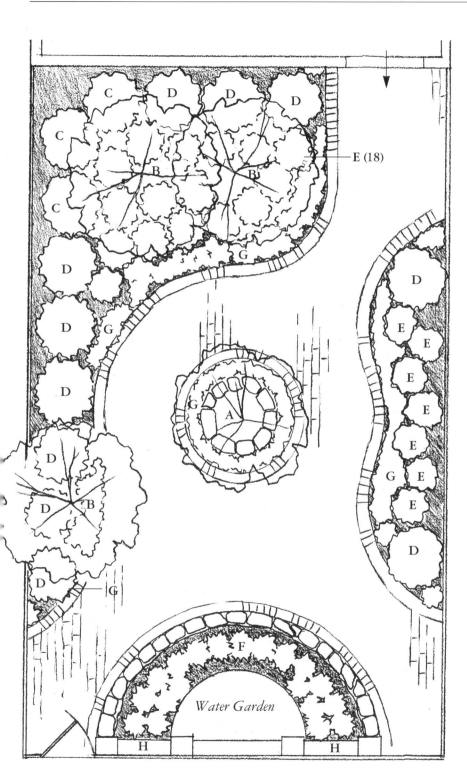

A. **Flowering Dogwood**
   (*Cornus florida*) (1)
      Note: Underplant
      dogwood with
      seasonal annuals.

B. **Eastern Redbud**
   (*Cercis canadensis*
   'Forest pansy')* (3)

C. **Koreanspice Viburnum**
   (*Viburnum carlesii*) (3)

D. **Boxwood**
   (*Buxus sempervirens*) (11)

E. **Azalea**
   (*Rhododendron,*
   Kurume hybrid,
   'Hinodegiri')* (25)

F. **Bog area of Siberian iris,**
   calla lilies and pickerel
   rush

G. **Seasonal bulbs and**
   annuals

H. **Sweet Autumn Clematis**
   on trellis
   (*Clematis ternata*) (2)

A Garden for Under a Deck

The space under a deck presents challenges in lightening the darkness and in dealing with support posts, but with careful attention to detail the area can yield a garden as pleasant to look at from within the house as out. In this design randomly laid stones keep with the informality of the wooden deck and provide clean transit from the back door to the rest of the garden. Ambitious gardeners may cultivate moss between the stones for a unique effect, or wrap the vertical support posts with chicken wire for vines like clematis or morning glories to climb. Ugly utilities are hidden behind an attractive lattice screen, a clever move for any garden.

Planned primarily for a vivid burst of spring color, flower colors center on purple, white and clear pink, but you may select white blooming varieties if you want to bring even more light into the space. Variegated liriope and white edged hosta further enhance and brighten the shaded space. Outside the window, a water garden acts as a focal point and is situated where it can be seen from inside.

A. **Rhododendron**
   (Rhododendron 'P.J.M.') (2)
B. **Azalea**
   (Rhododendron, Satsuki hybrid, Geisha') (3)
C. **Azalea**
   (Rhododendron, Girard hybrid, 'Renee Michelle') (4)
D. **English Boxwood**
   (Buxus sempervirens 'Suffruticosa') (7)
E. **Hosta underplanted with daffodil bulbs**
   (Hosta 'Francee') (3)
F. **Variegated Liriope**
   (Liriope muscari 'Variegata') (10)
G. **Pachysandra**
   (Pachysandra terminalis) (48)

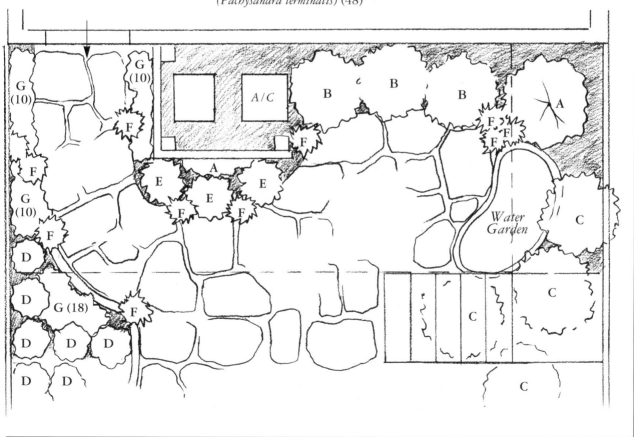

A Contemporary Garden

In the garden world some plants look exotic, unusual or sculptural, and there is no better place to showcase them than in a contemporary setting such as this. Planned around a distinctive garden pool the design provides for entertainment, relaxation and even something as practical as a tiny herb and salad plot behind the pool. When pondering the material for the floor of a contemporary space, plan for a simple design so it doesn't compete with all the "motion" created by the plants. In this plan, the paving is laid diagonally across the garden to create a feeling of spaciousness. Close to the house a stucco-covered wall conceals a service area for utilities, a potting bench and storage space. Placed diagonally across from the garden pool, it further continues the diagonal theme created by the paving.

As in many other gardens, the focal point of this garden is the pool, with its sleek lines and distinctive sculptural amphora fountain. Plants continue the contemporary theme and have been chosen for their highly artistic shapes. Large arching ornamental grasses complement sword-shaped flowers and foliage, while unusual trees and structural evergreens create year-round interest.

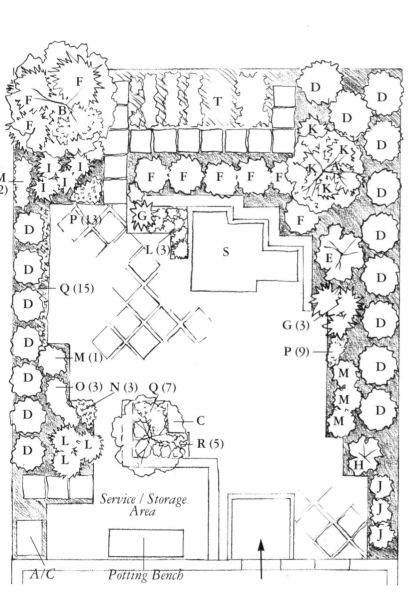

A. Smoke Tree
   (*Cotinus coggygria*) (1)
B. Goldenraintree
   (*Koelreuteria paniculata*) (1)
C. Flowering Dogwood
   (*Cornus florida*) (1)
D. Arborvitae
   (*Thuga occidentalis*) (17)
E. Maiden Grass
   (*Miscanthus sinensis*
   'Gracillimus') (1)
F. Cherry Laurel
   (*Prunus laurocerasus*
   'Otto Luykens') (9)
G. Yucca
   (*Yucca filementosa*) (4)
H. Leatherleaf Mahonia
   (*Mahonia bealei*) (1)
I. Red-Hot Poker
   (*Kniphofia uvaria*
   'Royal Standard') (4)
J. Compact Burning Bush
   (*Euonymus alata* 'Compacta') (3)
K. Juniper
   (*Juniperus horizontalis*
   'Plumosa Compacta') (4)
L. Fountain Grass
   (*Pennisetum alopeciroides*) (6)
M. Switchgrass
   (*Panicum virgatum*
   'Heavy Metal') (6)
N. Black-Eyed Susan
   (*Rudbeckia fulgida* 'Goldstrum') (3)
O. Sedum
   (*Sedum spectable* 'Autumn Joy') (3)
P. Pinks
   (*Dianthus gratianopolitanus*
   'Tiny Rubies') (22)
Q. Catmint
   (*Nepeta faasenii*) (22)
R. Dwarf Nandina
   (*Nandina domestica* 'Compacta') (5)
S. Pots of water iris, cattail
   and pickerel rush in pool.
T. Herb and salad garden
   behind pool.

A Fragrant Side Yard Garden

"End unit" or "side loading" townhouses have no adjoining residence at one side so they have more outdoor space for the gardener to "play" with. This design presents an entry door on the front of the house where foundation plantings blend across the driveway to a lovely side yard garden. Hard-working perennials combine with evergreen shrubs to create a small public entry garden while the side yard beyond the arbor is scented with pale-colored flowering plants that visually expand the narrow space and create a pleasant journey to the backyard. Perfumed aromas from such old-fashioned favorites as lilac, viburnum, honeysuckle, lemon lilies, iris and lily-of-the valley provide a sweet air that wafts up to the deck above, into the garden below and throughout the house when windows are thrown wide open on balmy days.

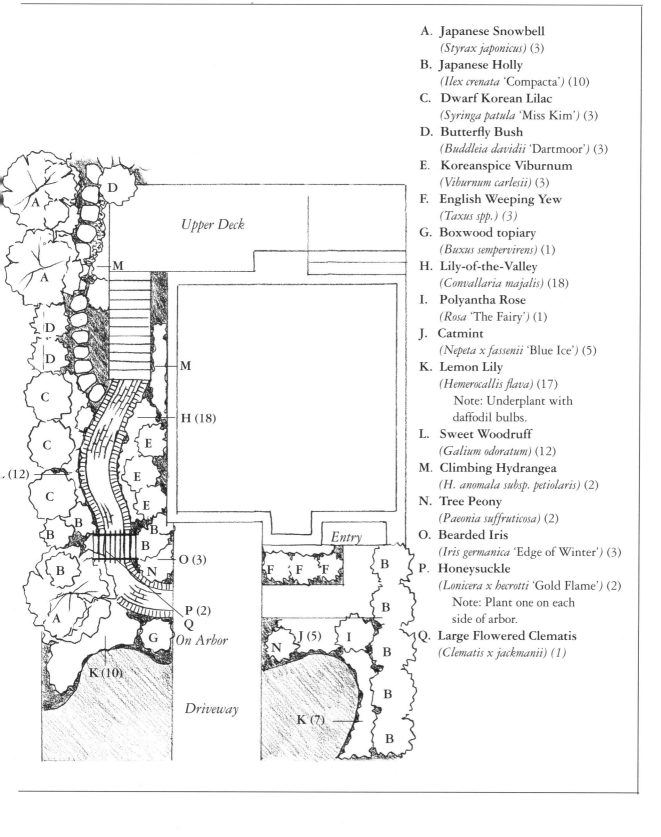

A. **Japanese Snowbell**
   (*Styrax japonicus*) (3)

B. **Japanese Holly**
   (*Ilex crenata* 'Compacta') (10)

C. **Dwarf Korean Lilac**
   (*Syringa patula* 'Miss Kim') (3)

D. **Butterfly Bush**
   (*Buddleia davidii* 'Dartmoor') (3)

E. **Koreanspice Viburnum**
   (*Viburnum carlesii*) (3)

F. **English Weeping Yew**
   (*Taxus spp.*) (3)

G. **Boxwood topiary**
   (*Buxus sempervirens*) (1)

H. **Lily-of-the-Valley**
   (*Convallaria majalis*) (18)

I. **Polyantha Rose**
   (*Rosa* 'The Fairy') (1)

J. **Catmint**
   (*Nepeta x fassenii* 'Blue Ice') (5)

K. **Lemon Lily**
   (*Hemerocallis flava*) (17)
   Note: Underplant with
   daffodil bulbs.

L. **Sweet Woodruff**
   (*Galium odoratum*) (12)

M. **Climbing Hydrangea**
   (*H. anomala subsp. petiolaris*) (2)

N. **Tree Peony**
   (*Paeonia suffruticosa*) (2)

O. **Bearded Iris**
   (*Iris germanica* 'Edge of Winter') (3)

P. **Honeysuckle**
   (*Lonicera x hecrotti* 'Gold Flame') (2)
   Note: Plant one on each
   side of arbor.

Q. **Large Flowered Clematis**
   (*Clematis x jackmanii*) (1)

A Garden for a Sloping Site

Because of the many rolling hills in the Mid-Atlantic region, slopes are a common challenge. Although they take up valuable space, slopes can usually be planted to provide the maximum amount of privacy in a townhouse yard. Slopes are natural noise buffers too, especially if your house is at the base of one. This design works well whether your slope goes down-hill or up. Close to the house, an interesting curved brick patio has been planned for entertainment, relaxation and to make maximum use of the flattest area of the yard.

Plants are placed so they create an appealing privacy screen, shielding the patio from neighboring townhouses behind the lot. Spring brings the garden into its glory with blossoms of dark pink, white and light pink that complement the bright green of the pachysandra groundcover. In the summer a mass of pink flowering perennial begonias and a variegated hydrangea brighten up the garden while cool season structure is held by the groundcover, cherry laurels and nandina surrounding the patio.

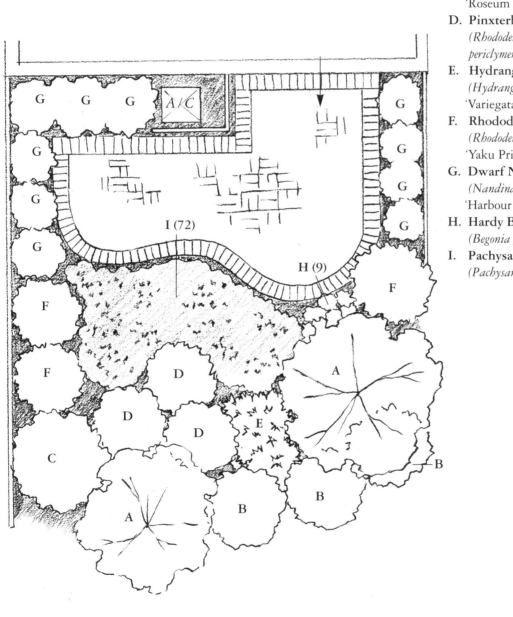

A. **Eastern Redbud**
   (Cercis canadensis) (2)
B. **Cherry Laurel**
   (Prunus laurocerasus
   'Otto Luyken') (3)
C. **Rhododendron**
   (Rhododendron catawbiense
   'Roseum Elegans') (1)
D. **Pinxterbloom Azalea**
   (Rhododendron
   periclymenoides) (3)
E. **Hydrangea**
   (Hydrangea macrophylla
   'Variegata') (1)
F. **Rhododendron**
   (Rhododendron yakusimanum
   'Yaku Princess') (3)
G. **Dwarf Nandina**
   (Nandina domestica
   'Harbour Dwarf') (10)
H. **Hardy Begonia**
   (Begonia grandis) (9)
I. **Pachysandra**
   (Pachysandra terminalis) (72)

A Birdwatcher's Garden

Though clearly designed to attract wildlife, this garden also accommodates the human element quite well with an informal patio and walkway of irregularly patterned, dry-laid flagstone slabs that lead from the back door around a curved planting to a small, private patio area. Strolling along the walkway one notices the four necessities for attracting wildlife to the garden: food, water, cover and nesting sites. Feeders and berry-producing shrubs provide food, while water is provided with a low bowl and a splashing wall fountain. A nesting box and deciduous trees furnish valuable places for birds to raise their young and a wealth of vegetation provides much-needed cover and protection from predators.

Shady areas under the trees are taken up with textural plants that are pleasing to look at throughout the growing season. Shown as shaded areas on the landscape plan, specific plants are not laid out on the design, but instead the planting of these areas is interpretive and meant to be filled the way the gardener wishes.

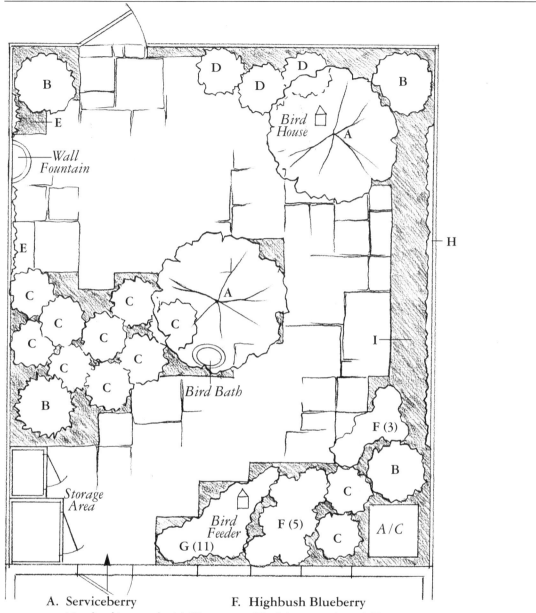

A. Serviceberry
   (*Amelanchier canadensis*) (2)

B. Foster Holly
   (*Ilex x attenuata* 'Fosteri') (4)

C. Inkberry
   (*Ilex glabra* 'Shamrock') (11)

D. American Cranberrybush Viburnum
   (*V. trilobum* 'Compactum') (3)

E. Pyracantha Espalier
   (*Pyracantha coccinea*) (2)

F. Highbush Blueberry
   (*Vaccinium corymbosum*) (8)

G. Black-eyed Susan
   (*Rudbeckia fulgida* 'Goldstrum') (11)

H. Virginia Creeper on wall
   (*Parthenocissus quinquefolia*) (1)

I. Shady areas for perennials:
   hosta, ferns, astilbe, cardinal flower, ajuga, Solomon's seal and woodland phlox.

A Garden for Hummingbirds and Butterflies

Butterflies and hummingbirds are delicate creatures that are easy to attract with borders full of the nectar-rich flowers they love. Suitable for an open, sunny site, this design includes a wide variety of perennials and annuals that these animated creatures of summer will flock to.

Hummingbirds prefer bright, tubular flowers that can be probed for nectar and are especially attracted to vibrant colors like scarlet, orange and red. They also love to shower in the mist created by a misting feature on a birdbath. Stores specializing in wild bird feeding will be able to suggest one for your garden, as well as sell you a hummingbird feeder. Nectar that you mix yourself (one part sugar to four parts water, no coloring added) can be offered and should be changed at least weekly. Butterflies are also attracted to flowers rich in nectar, as well as to fennel and parsley which they need in their caterpillar stage.

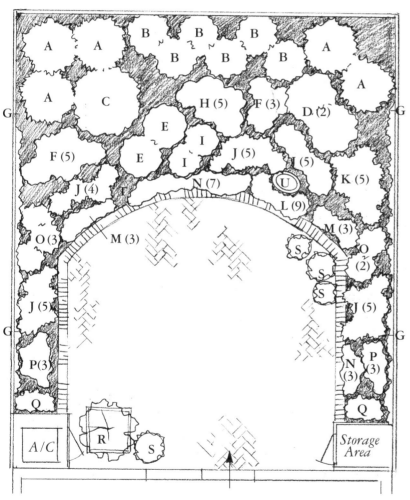

A. **Foster Holly**
   (*Ilex x attenuata* 'Fosterii') (5)

B. **Yew**
   (*Taxus x media* 'Hicksii') (6)

C. **Butterfly Bush**
   (*Buddleia davidii* 'Black Knight') (1)

D. **Joe Pye Weed**
   (*Eupatorium maculatum* 'Gateway') (2)

E. **Red-Hot Poker**
   (*Kniphofia uvaria* 'Alcazar') (2)

F. **Foxglove**
   (*Digitalis purpurea*) (8)

G. **Trumpet Honeysuckle**
   (*Lonicera sempervirens*) (4)

H. **Blue Cardinal Flower**
   (*Lobelia siphilitica*) (5)

I. **Yarrow**
   (*Achillia filipendulina* 'Coronation Gold') (2)

J. **Purple Coneflowers**
   (*Echinacea purpurea*) (24)

K. **Bee Balm**
   (*Monarda didyma* 'Cambridge Scarlet') (5)

L. **Parsley**
   (*Petroselinum hortense*) (9)

M. **Coreopsis**
   (*Coreopsis verticillata* 'Moonbeam') (6)

N. **Butterfly Weed**
   (*Asclepias tuberosa*) (10)

O. **Daylily**
   (*Hemerocallis* 'Happy Returns') (5)

P. **Fennel**
   (*Foeniculum vulgare*) (6)

Q. **Hollyhock**
   (*Alcea rosea* 'Old Farmyard') (2)

R. **Tropical Hibiscus Tree**
   (*Hibiscus rosa-sinensis*) (1)

S. **Annual Red Salvia in pots on patio**
   (*Salvia splendens*)

T. **Hummingbird Feeder**

U. **Bird Bath with Misting Feature**

An End-Unit Front Yard

Proving that gardens are prettier than a lot of grass, this front garden uses textural foliage interest to transform a long entry into a place of beauty and repose. Designed for varied seasonal interest, the garden is as pretty to look at from inside the house as it is from the outside. A grassy effect is created with perennial liriope to give the flavor of a small lawn without all the upkeep.

The garden comes to life in the spring when azaleas, viburnums, bulbs and ajuga bloom. Summer brings the flowering of hosta, liriope and the lovely stewartia tree, a "multi-season" specimen with large white summer flowers, colorful fall leaves and exfoliating winter bark. In the cooler months when herbaceous plants are dormant, evergreens like holly and yew work with the gently curved rock wall to provide structure to the design.

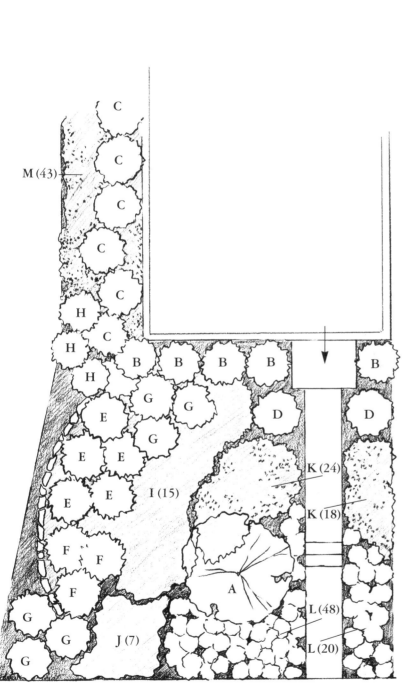

A. **Japanese Stewartia**
   (Stewartia pseudocamellia) (1)

B. **Japanese Holly**
   (Ilex crenata 'Compacta') (5)

C. **Dwarf Burford Holly**
   (Ilex cornuta 'Dwarf Burford') (6)

D. **English Weeping Yew**
   (Taxis spp.) (2)

E. **American Cranberrybush Viburnum**
   (V. trilobum 'Compactum') (5)

F. **Azalea**
   (Rhododendron, Girard Hybrid, 'Renee Michelle') (3)

G. **Leucothoe**
   (Leucothoe fontanesiana 'Girard's Rainbow') (6)

H. **Hosta**
   (Hosta 'Gold Standard') (3)

I. **Hosta**
   (Hosta 'Honeybells', 'Francee', 'Gold Standard') (15)

J. **Hosta**
   (Hosta 'Golden Tiara') (7)

K. **Ajuga**
   (Ajuga reptans 'Bronze Beauty') (42)

L. **Variegated Liriope**
   (Liriope muscari 'Variegata') (68)

M. **Periwinkle**
   (Vinca minor) (48)

A Deck-Top Garden

Raised decks that are perched high in the air should contain numerous containers overflowing with plants, not only to soften the harsh architectural lines of the deck, but to make an inviting transition from the inside of the house to the outside. This spacious deck design shows 18 containers of varying sizes that give the effect of a garden in the sky. Containers of graduated sizes are planted so as to overflow in abundance and are placed in groups around the deck, under the pergola structure created to provide an airy sense of enclosure and privacy.

I do not want to suggest particular plants for your containers here except to say that you should refer to Chapter Seven.

Seven for ideas. Container gardening, like decorating, is subjective. I would no sooner tell you what color your draperies should be than tell you what, specifically, you should plant in your container gardens. These are part of the "decoration" of the deck and the color and arrangement of flowers are a matter of artistry. I would suggest, however, that container gardens be changed seasonally—-planted and replanted with fresh things as the seasons progress.

Deck-top gardens require vigorous watering, almost daily in windy or sultry summer conditions. And because the water washes through the soil and out the hole in the bottom of the pot, plants should be fed regularly with a water-soluble fertilizer. Flowering annuals can be kept producing and bushy by pinching or snipping leggy growth. The only other maintenance consists of protecting your investment in the deck. Treat the wood with suitable cleaners and preservatives annually.

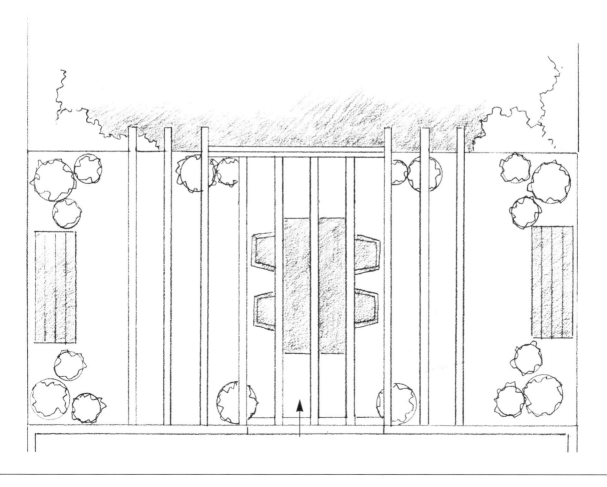

A Tiny Townhouse Garden

This intimate "courtyard" might be found at the back of any city rowhouse or townhouse. Minimal in size, such a plot is often thought of as useless, but well planned and executed landscapes can transform such a tiny neglected space into an intimate garden sanctuary. This elegant, albeit small, landscape focuses on an exquisite wall fountain, pool and patio. The fountain, a verdigris "tree of life", is mounted on a column of brick at the boundary wall that surrounds a patio adequately sized for a small cafe table and chairs.

The plants that accent the space have been chosen for visual appeal and year-round interest. Foliage and flower colors were chosen to enhance the burgundy leaves of the Japanese maple. In the spring, bright red-violet azalea flowers combine with the dogwood and purple ajuga blossoms, beautifully accenting the brickwork and foliage of the maple and pieris. In the summer, color comes from daylilies, water lilies and from pots filled with flowering annuals on the patio. Throughout the cooler months structural plants like pyracantha and spruce hold the composition together.

A. **Flowering Dogwood**
   (Cornus florida) (1)

B. **Smooth Hydrangea**
   (Hydrangea arborescens 'Annabelle') (1)

C. **Japanese Maple**
   (Acer palmatum 'Bloodgood') (1)

D. **Azalea**
   (Rhodendron, Kurume
   hybrid, 'Hino Crimson') (3)

E. **Pieris**
   (Pieris japonica 'Mountain Fire') (3)

F. **Dwarf Alberta Spruce**
   (Picea glauca 'Conica') (1)

G. **Pyracantha Espalier**
   (Pyracantha coccinea) (2)

H. **Climbing Hydrangea**
   (H. anomala subsp. petiolaris) (1)

I. **Daylily**
   (Hemerocallis 'Stella D'Oro') (2)

J. **Ajuga**
   (Ajuga reptans 'Bronze Beauty') (43)

K. **Epimedium**
   (Epimedium x rubrum) (5)

L. **Water Lily**
   (Nymphaea hybrid) (2)

M. **Containers with seasonal annuals**

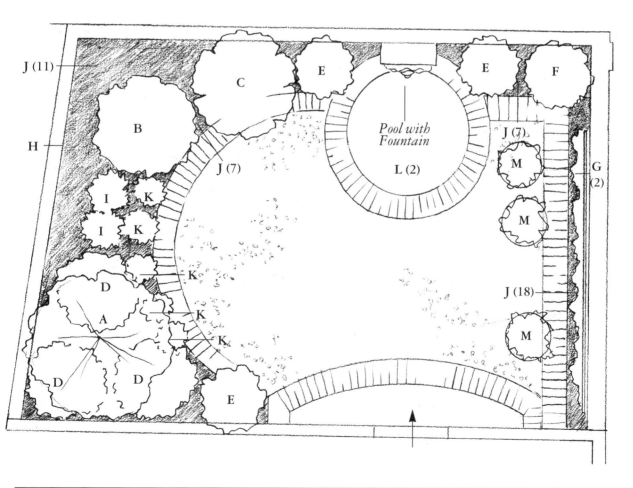

A Shady Garden

This design for a long, narrow space, contains a potting shed and a second story deck for entertainment. Interesting plants make a pretty picture of texture and foliage when viewed from the elevated deck, and are appealing enough to invite exploration. Under the deck, a flagstone landing leads from the back door to a green swath of grass that winds through the backyard.

The length of the space is broken by bringing the plantings well out into the middle space of the garden in deep, S-shaped borders. This creates more mystery than straight beds along the length of the fence. There is a sense of wonder at what lies beyond, which is desirable in small, narrow gardens.

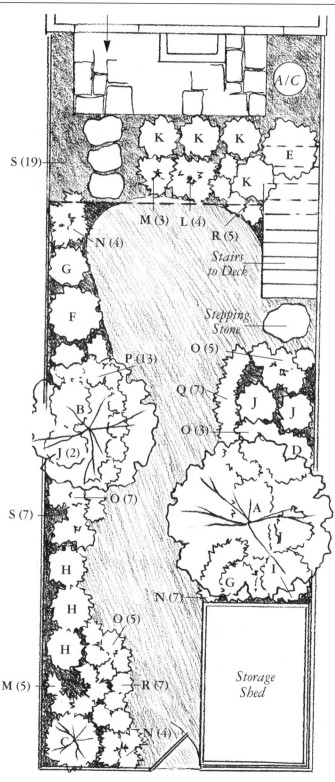

A. **River Birch**
   (Betula nigra 'Heritage'*)* (1)

B. **Flowering Dogwood**
   (Cornus florida 'Cherokee'*)* (1)

C. **Hicks Yew**
   (Taxus x media 'Hicksii'*)* (1)

D. **Judd Viburnum**
   (Viburnum x juddii) (1)

E. **Rhododendron**
   (Rhododendron
   'Boule de Neige'*)* (1)

F. **Oakleaf Hydrangea**
   (Hydrangea quercifolia
   'PeeWee'*)* (1)

G. **Nandina**
   (Nandina domestica) (2)

H. **Red-Twig Dogwood**
   (Cornus sericea) (3)

I. **Pieris**
   (Pieris japonica) (1)

J. **Leucothoe**
   (Leucothoe fontanesiana
   'Girards Rainbow'*)* (5)

K. **Azalea**
   (Rhododendron, Kurume hybrid,
   'Coral Bells'*)* (4)

L. **Hosta**
   (Hosta fortunei
   'Aureo-marginata'*)* (4)

M. **Hosta**
   (Hosta x 'Royal Standard'*)* (8)

N. **Japanese Painted Fern**
   (Athyrium nipponicum
   'Pictum'*)* (15)

O. **Astilbe**
   (Astilbe japonica 'Europa'*)* (20)

P. **Siberian Iris**
   (Iris siberica) (13)

Q. **Daylily**
   (Hemerocallis
   (*'Happy Returns'*)* (7)

R. **Coral Bells**
   (Heuchera americana
   'Palace Purple'*)* (12)

S. **Liriope**
   (Liriope muscari) (26)

The KinderGarden

To encourage a child in a garden is to nurture the next generation of gardeners. In this garden children can explore the magical transformation that seeds make as they grow into plants. They can exercise, make believe, have picnics and receive an education on the wonders of nature. Here a poured concrete pathway, aptly named the "trike track", takes center stage while a sunny circle of lawn encourages picnics and cloud watching. The playhouse encourages inventive gametime. Artistic children can create masterpieces on stepping stones or on a chalkboard mounted on the rear gate.

Children will love attracting songbirds, butterflies and hummingbirds with plants, feeders, a birdbath and nesting box. They can dig in the earth to plant annuals like sunflowers, parsley and more flowers in the window boxes of the playhouse. Strawberries and blueberries can be picked and eaten in the summer, if birds don't get to them first! This is also the time when honeysuckle flowers can be harvested for the single, sweet drop of nectar that all children love.

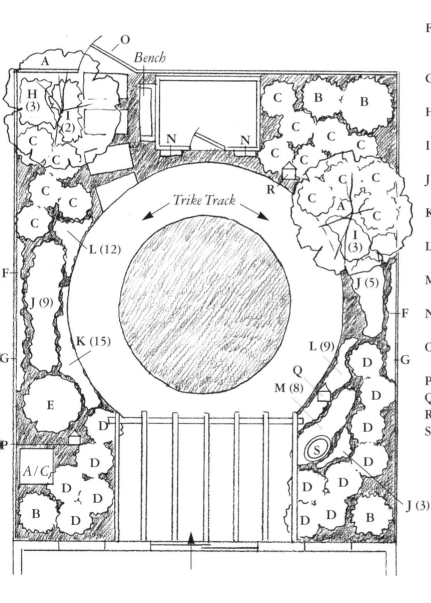

A. **Serviceberry**
   (*Amelanchier canadensis*) (2)
B. **Foster Holly**
   (*Ilex x attenuata* 'Fosteri') (4)
C. **Inkberry**
   (*Ilex glabra* 'Shamrock') (15)
D. **Blueberry**
   (*Vaccinium corymbosum*) (13)
E. **Dwarf Butterfly Bush**
   (*Buddleia davidii* 'Lochinch') (1)
F. **Honeysuckle**
   (*Lonicera x hecrotti*
   'Gold Flame') (2)
G. **Clematis**
   (*Clematis* 'The President') (2)
H. **Astilbe**
   (*Astilbe x arendisii* 'Fanal') (3)
I. **Hosta**
   (*Hosta* 'Patriot') (5)
J. **Sunflowers**
   (*Helianthus annuus*) (17)
K. **Alpine Strawberries**
   (*Fragaria*) (15)
L. **Parsley**
   (*Petroselinum hortense*) (21)
M. **Black-eyed Susans**
   (*Rudbeckia fulgida* 'Goldstrum') (8)
N. **Window boxes of flowering**
   annuals
O. **Chalkboard mounted on gate**
   for sidewalk chalk
P. **Hummingbird feeder**
Q. **Seed feeder for birds**
R. **Nest box for birds**
S. **Bird Bath/Splash Fountain**

A Low-Maintenance Backyard

Here low maintenance is the goal with a design that focuses on structural features like the patio paving and fountain, and easy-care shrubs, groundcovers and climbers. The garden accommodates a slight change of slope with a curving step down to a dining area, but if you do not have a slope, you may eliminate the step in the design and keep the formal flagstone patio on one level.

Plants have been well chosen to provide for ease of care as well as for four seasons of interest. In the winter, evergreen boxwood, mahonia and sculptural cotoneaster hold the structure of the garden together while spring brings color in the form of the flowering redbud trees and can be made even more interesting by planting bulbs amid the groundcovering pachysandra. In summer, blossoms from the hydrangea will brighten the space while flowering water plants accent the main focal point of the space, the small ornamental pool and fountain. In the autumn, interest comes from colorful foliage of redbuds and hydrangea and from berries on the mahonia and cotoneaster.

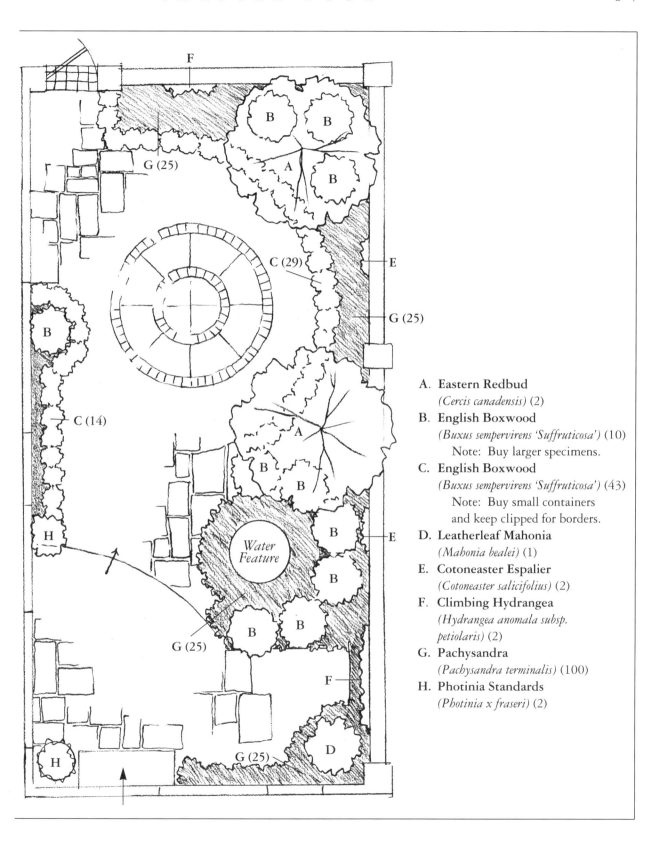

A. **Eastern Redbud**
   (Cercis canadensis) (2)

B. **English Boxwood**
   (Buxus sempervirens 'Suffruticosa') (10)
   Note: Buy larger specimens.

C. **English Boxwood**
   (Buxus sempervirens 'Suffruticosa') (43)
   Note: Buy small containers
   and keep clipped for borders.

D. **Leatherleaf Mahonia**
   (Mahonia bealei) (1)

E. **Cotoneaster Espalier**
   (Cotoneaster salicifolius) (2)

F. **Climbing Hydrangea**
   *(Hydrangea anomala subsp.
   petiolaris)* (2)

G. **Pachysandra**
   (Pachysandra terminalis) (100)

H. **Photinia Standards**
   (Photinia x fraseri) (2)

A Cottage Garden of Edibles

Though not capable of supplying the dietary needs of an entire family, this garden promises a wealth of delicious berries, herbs, edible flowers and unusual vegetables right outside the back door. The main focal point is the potting shed, a charming, yet useful centerpiece that lends a cottage-like atmosphere to the garden. This is presented within a diagonal design that creates a sense of spaciousness and allows for intensive planting techniques. Windowboxes and containers are also used for strawberries, flowers and tender herbs like rosemary which often must be wintered indoors.

The patio, laid in a merry blend of brick and flagstone pavers, creates a quilt-like informality in keeping with the tone set by the potting shed. Two "raised" beds provide space for vegetables and salad greens. Dwarf fruit trees create vertical interest and at the same time allow for ladder-free harvesting of fruit. A serviceberry tree also yields berries that are delicious when baked into pies while blueberries and gooseberries round out the gastronomically useful shrubbery.

A. **Dwarf Apple Trees**
   (Malus pumila) (2)
B. **Dwarf Nectarine Tree**
   (Prunus persica) (1)
C. **Serviceberry**
   (Amelanchier canadensis) (1)
D. **Gooseberry**
   (Ribes spp.) (2)
E. **Dwarf Peach Tree**
   (Prunus persica) (1)
F. **Asparagus Bed**
   (Asparagus officinalis) (6)
G. **Arborvitae**
   (Thuga occidentalis) (5)

H. **Highbush Blueberries**
   (Vaccinium corymbosum) (14)
      Note: Plant at least two
      varieties for adequate cross-
      pollination.
I. **Raised bed for salad greens**
J. **Raised bed for vegetables**
K. **Herbs and edible flowers:**
   *violets, nasturtiums, alpine
   strawberries, thyme, oregano, basil,
   chives, sage and others.*
L. **Grapes on fence and against
   house wall**
   (Vitus spp.) (3)

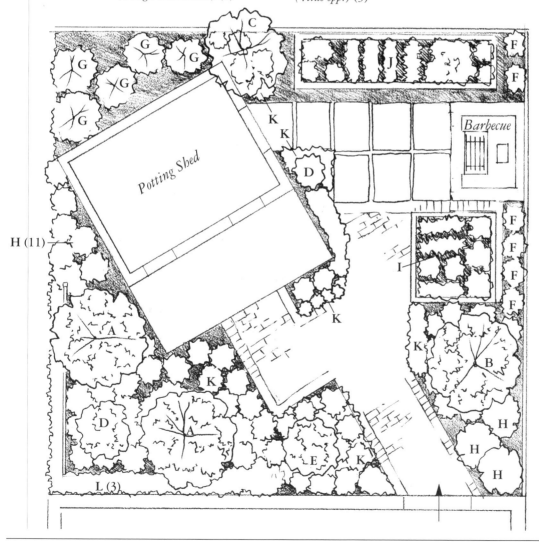

5.

Hardscapes

"Hardscape" is the term most landscape designers use for the floor and structures of the garden. Patios, decks and other outdoor floors are most commonly referred to as the "hardscape", but other structures such as pergolas, arbors, walls, fences and gazebos are considered part of the overall hardscape as well. Because they are major forces in the design, they must be carefully planned. These important "bones of the garden" will literally carry the garden during the winter time.

The Floor of Your Garden

You'll spend most of your time on the "floor" of your garden. You'll sit on it, stand on it, relax on furniture set on it, entertain on it, look at it all year long and put more wear on it than any other feature in the garden. For this reason, choosing the material that makes up the floor is the most important decision you'll make. The hard surface will probably take up more room than the planting areas and it will probably be the single most expensive item that you install in the garden.

Patios and decking take up more space because they are essential to the human use of the garden space. These hard spaces need to be attractive, durable, level, easy to clean, weed-free and complementary to the house. The floor of your garden should integrate the overall landscape with the house and create a transition zone from the inside to the outside. If well chosen and installed, hard surfaces make the most valuable contribution to the garden because they are constant—365 days a year.

With all this riding on it, you'd think more people would choose their outdoor flooring more carefully. Instead, as soon as the mortgage papers are signed, a contractor is seen nailing up a deck that partly obscures, or even completely conceals, most of the valuable ground space of the townhouse. Often the back of whole blocks of neighborhood townhouses consists of second-story decks abutting one another in a long line of protruding outdoor platforms that nobody ever seems to inhabit.

Wood decking has experienced a Renaissance of sorts in suburban communities around the country. Its popularity has soared because pressure treated wood resists rot for a long period of time, it's inexpensive, it provides a level living surface where the ground is steep and it's easy to work with. Almost anyone who can wield a hammer can build a deck, but decking has its drawbacks.

First, pressure treated wood has come under the scrutiny of environmentalists for the toxicity of the chemicals that are used to treat it. Some worry that the arsenic-like chemicals that impregnate the wood will leach away and poison the soil. The literature that accompanies pressure treated wood even cautions against breathing in the dust generated when the stuff is cut. This is a serious consideration when you're growing your own food in raised timber beds, building your own deck or if you have kids and pets playing on the wood often. And though pressure treated wood is cheap initially, it ends up costing more in the long run when it needs to be treated year after year with preservatives and sealers—a costly, time consuming and messy proposition.

One of the main complaints about wood decking is that wood splinters as it ages. This is a big problem for anyone who wants to lounge barefoot on the deck. The nature of these wood "beasts" is that decking is biodegradable. It must have very regular maintenance to stay livable. Wood is, after all, a natural substance and even the best built decks will eventually deteriorate and crumble to the ground.

Now with all that said, you might think that I really hate wood decks; I do dislike them to a certain degree. They are much too commonly used when another material would suffice. They are hard to design around when towering above the garden—making one feel that they are perched above the landscape rather than being an active part of it. Aesthetically speaking, they often don't "fit" the style of the house they are attached to. Homeowners tend to build them too big and they obscure much of the valuable soil underneath that could be used for planting beautiful things. Also, many elevated decks are unlivable spaces because they offer no shelter from the scorching sun and no privacy from neighbors—especially when the neighbors own a deck within inches of yours.

Wood decking is a logical choice, however, when you have no flat land to live on. Cantilevering a deck over a steep slope brings you closer to nature, like a bird in a tree if you're lucky enough to have a forest sitting right outside your back door. Why build one if you don't have a steep grade or a forest of trees? Why not pave the center of your garden with an attractive, no-maintenance stone or brick patio, plant small trees for privacy and draw attention to the inward sanctuary of your garden?

Right now you might be saying, "But I have this door leading from the dining room (or living room or whatever room...) on the second level of my townhouse. What do I put outside that door?" I agree that you should have some sort of structure there. Perhaps a small balcony, tied back into the house wall without huge posts sunk into the ground beneath, would suit your desire to throw open the doors and step outside on a sunny day. You could place a cafe set there for the morning breakfast to visually expand the interior of your townhome without detracting from the garden below. The garden would still be the main focus of the yard; in fact you would have a wonderful vantage point from which to view the greenery below.

Larger decks should have a staircase that leads to the garden below. The stairs invite exploration and a lower patio area acts as a welcome mat of sorts that the garden revolves around. For a real architectural statement, consider a circular staircase. These are beautiful additions to any elevated deck and save valuable space in small gardens.

Wood decking is only one of many highly useful materials available for the floor of your garden. The surfaces that enhance gardens the best are natural ones. Handsome cut stone, brick aged with the patina of time or field stones interplanted with creeping mosses and herbs make the garden appear mature and soften the garden's "newness". Newer interlocking pavers are also beautiful in small doses and can be laid in many patterns. These pavers can be laid intricately to look almost like an Oriental carpet or simply like a tiled floor. The possibilities are endless.

The materials that enhance gardens the best are classic, aged well or old looking. I'd much rather have a few square feet of classic flagstone than an entire yard full of decking. Classic stone materials are relatively easy to install in a bed of stone dust or sand, but you may wish to turn mortar jobs over to a skilled mason.

Be ruthless and picky in choosing the floor of your garden. If your heart is set on flagstone and you're living with concrete, find the means to have the flagstone, even if you can only have a small area of it. Don't compromise, for you may regret it later.

A balcony provides an interesting alternative to the obtrusiveness of a large deck. The entire yard can then be utilized as a garden.

Keep the character of the garden in mind throughout the selection process and choose a material that keeps with your garden theme and personal style. Perhaps you love contemporary lines and have a piece of abstract sculpture for the garden. Your modern taste calls for a flooring material of the same nature—frost free tiles perhaps or square flagstone pavers set in mortar would look great on the floor of your garden. Conversely, if you long for a flower filled cottage, then your paving choice might lean more towards the casual—bricks laid in sand in a basketweave design or flat fieldstones interplanted with moss with bent willow "twig" furniture to complement all your blowzy, flowering plants.

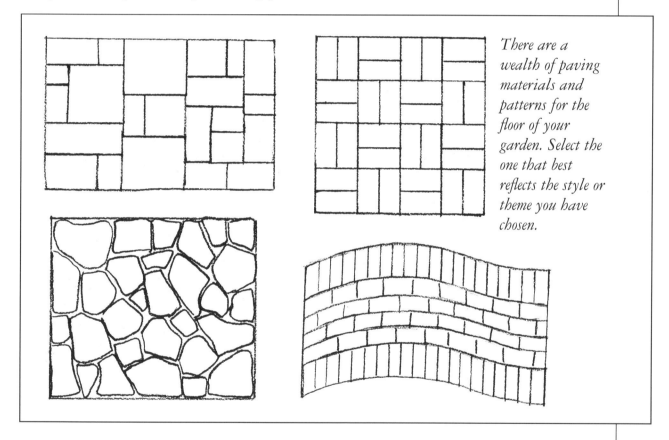

There are a wealth of paving materials and patterns for the floor of your garden. Select the one that best reflects the style or theme you have chosen.

The floor of your garden should complement the style you've chosen and be the stage for all the plantings, other structures and accessories that are to follow. If you're short on cash and cannot afford the hard material of your dream, consider plain pea gravel set within borders of timber or bricks. Gravel is an inexpensive alternative to grass and offers an excellent level surface for living in informal gardens. Pea gravel is usually the best and most comfortable to walk on, and it can yield small pockets that plants can actually grow in.

When paving stones are laid without mortar, the joints can then be used to grow a wide variety of small plants. This practice can make a new garden feel mature.

The list of outdoor flooring options is almost endless. Wood decking, brick, flagstone, interlocking pavers, concrete, aggregate, stamped concrete, thin pavers, frost-proof tiles, gravel, field stones and just about anything that can be imbedded in mortar, grouted in place or laid in a bed of sand or stone dust will work. Take time to visit several stone yards in your area before deciding upon the best material for your garden. It pays to bring samples home for comparison in the natural light of your own garden. What looks right at the nursery or stone yard may not look right against your own house.

When making your selections, consider the color and scale of the paving material. Smaller individual paving pieces usually show better in small spaces than larger slabs of stone. Remember, proportion is important and large pieces are not usually in scale to small gardens. Additionally, smaller pieces are easier to handle and simplify installation.

Pattern is also important to consider. If you're planning to have many textures and colors in the plantings, it might be best to have a simple floor. Conversely, if you prefer a less colorful atmosphere, you may choose a more complex pattern in the flooring to keep the space interesting. Be careful to coordinate the flooring material with your style and with other components of the garden. It's generally best to use no more than two or three materials for flooring and other structures. Every element should not compete for attention.

Great material combinations that work well in small townhouse gardens include brick with wood, flagstone with iron, and field stones with natural bark. These combinations speak of a style all their own and can be used for many features in the garden. Perhaps you already have a wooden privacy fence; if so, brick might be a suitable companion as a patio. Add a teak garden bench and suitable plantings in terra cotta pots to match the patina of the brick and wood and you're in business. Maybe you own a flagstone patio. You might then accessorize with classic black iron furniture, or in the case of the field stones, use shredded bark to lay paths through a casual planting of shade loving plants nestled beneath the canopy of a small grove of trees.

Siting the Floor

Most homeowners site the floor of their gardens right outside the back door. This makes sense if your garden is facing inward and has no desirable view outside its four walls. If you're facing a beautiful view, however, you may want to place your patio away from the house at the outer border of the property so you can enjoy the scenery. A small landing will suffice outside the back door, and stepping stones may be used to lead to the patio area beyond.

In formal gardens beautiful flooring might go from the door and flow to the middle space of the garden. Surround this with raised stone beds that are overflowing with plants and the garden will look stunning. The key is to site the patio where it will be used the most. Study the path of the sun in your garden to help determine the best place for the floor. You want to put it where it's best suited to your needs. There isn't a law that says you have to put the patio right outside the back door.

Vertical Interest

Just like our houses, our gardens should have walls and ceilings. These often overlooked elements contribute greatly to the ambiance of our outdoor environments. According to Thomas Jefferson, one of the greatest gardeners this country has ever known, good fences make good neighbors. Fences also provide privacy, security and an opportunity to shut out unpleasant surroundings. By themselves, though, tall privacy fences are oppressive and can easily dominate the entire landscape.

In the front yard, a picket or low iron fence surrounding an entry garden is charming and delineates the property nicely. In backyard gardens, however, where views are good, consider lowering the fence height so the garden is contained but the view is not lost. You may even "frame up" the view with trees planted on either side of the garden to bring the desired picture into more prominence. This is called "borrowing the view" and makes the garden seem more spacious.

Fences and garden walls provide vertical opportunities to the gardener. When well obscured by plants or clothed in vines, they soften the atmosphere and give us cause to lift our eyes upward to the garden's ceiling. Plain walls can be dressed up with panels of lattice that vines are allowed to clamber up. You may further accent the panels by cutting out decorative "nooks" in the shape of a circle or diamond where special pieces of garden art can be displayed. Fences and garden walls also provide an opportunity to display art. Wall mounted fountains, planted wire baskets, decorative plaques or even a collection of birdhouses can create a focal point on walls that are softened with vines and climbing plants.

The Garden Skyline

The ceiling of your garden might consist of overhead structures such as a patio roof, arbor, pergola, awning, overhang, gazebo roof or even a canopy of trees—the most natural and beautiful of all ceilings. Whether consisting of trees or vine covered structures, ceilings provide privacy from overlooking windows and can shelter patios from the harsh sun.

Overhead structures such as pergolas are always more useful when covered in vines such as grapes, Virginia creeper or wisteria. Be aware that grapes hang down from vines atop garden structures and plan for extra height when constructing overhead structures to avoid hitting them every time you walk under. Wisteria too is guilty of claiming airspace under pergolas when it blooms in the spring. Though beautiful and highly scented, the dangling flower clusters are a favorite visiting place for bees and other stingers, so be sure to include extra headroom for those times when the vine blossoms. Vigorous growers such as wisteria and trumpet vine are capable of taking down any structure supported by less than 6 by 6 posts. These climbers have a sheer will to dominate so it pays to only grow them only on the sturdiest of supports. Indeed, it pays to know the mature size and clinging power of any plant you are attempting to train to overhead supports before you dig.

TOWNHOUSE TIP

If you want to change ugly concrete, but cannot afford the high price of brick, consider laying a border of brick (in what is called a, "soldier course") around the existing concrete slab. This automatically dresses up the area and adds a few more inches to the size of the patio. Dress up the area with beautiful furniture and lush container gardens and the ugly concrete will be less noticeable. Also to coordinate even further, consider using more bricks to build pathways, edge walkways, build a barbecue, make raised beds or create a water feature.

6.

Plants for the Townhouse Garden

*P*lants are the reason most of us begin digging around a garden in the first place. Trees, shrubs, vines, grasses, perennials, annuals and groundcovers soften the hard lines of architecture and create a leafy oasis where we can relax and find solace from the world. Garden structures like arbors and fences seem austere when standing alone, but when obscured by plants, they soften visually. In small gardens, plants should contribute to the year-round appeal of the space. This is an important consideration because the space takes center stage and is on view at all times. Plants must be selected for their continuing good looks.

To plan for several seasons of interest, use a mix of evergreens, small trees, deciduous flowering shrubs, perennials, annuals, grasses, vines, groundcovers and bulbs. Evergreen shrubs fill the bill nicely for year-round interest, but can become overwhelming and too funereal if overused. As in achieving a balance in structures and plants, and the open spaces between them (mass and void), you must strive to balance the types of plants you choose. Choose evergreens for their "faithful", verdant appearance, but strive to balance them with interesting deciduous plants as well. In the summer flowering perennials and annuals fill the bill, but trees, shrubs and ornamental grasses provide a second interest level in autumn when their leaves turn bright crimson or gold. This lends another aspect to the ever-changing garden picture.

Many deciduous shrubs are appealing throughout the year. Autumnal color comes from the foliage of burning bush and blueberries, and with berries from viburnums and cotoneaster. For winter interest try red-twig dogwood with its striking bark color or the vibrant berries of winterberry. In the spring early bloomers such as Japanese pieris, dwarf rhododendrons, viburnums and azaleas flower along with tulips and daffodils; and for summer look to the lushness of roses and butterfly bushes. Interesting variegated foliage from variegated holly or gold-flecked aucuba always looks good and is always welcome in small gardens. Groundcovers too, will do double duty year-round to suppress weeds while providing a good looking covering to the bare soil around major plantings.

The Individuality of the Site

New gardeners often get confused when they set out to buy plants for the garden. They are apt to be seduced by what looks great at the nursery rather than by what will ultimately do best in their gardens. At the very least you should make your selections based on the available sunlight in your garden. It's easy to gauge if the yard is shady or sunny and plants may be bought based on this simple assessment. But, just as there are many plants to choose from, there are many differing types of light. Perhaps your shade comes from buildings, not from trees. Buildings create a dense, almost dark shade that many plants cannot survive in. The same is true of the shade under trees such as maples. Not only is their shade dense, the greedy roots of maples grasp every available inch of surface soil, leaving a dry, dirt-like environment where little will grow. It can get confusing. The sun may be bright and hot from a southern exposure or mild from the early morning sunrise. The shade may be dappled through a canopy of trees or light enough that even sun lovers like daylilies will grow nicely. Typically, if you have morning sun and shade in the afternoon, you'll have a situation where most shade lovers will grow. If you have morning shade and afternoon sun, you'll have to choose sun loving plants because the sun is more intense later in the day.

Right Plant, Right Place

To begin the process of plant selection you must again turn to the site. Look over your original site notes. Examine the path of the sun as it moves across the yard during the day and evaluate the quality of the soil. Though the soil quality can be easily adjusted, it takes substantial work to alter sunlight in the garden. Trees can be planted, "limbed up" or eliminated entirely to change the amount of sun your garden gets, but other features are less easily modified. Gusty winds and dry soil from building overhangs are usually more difficult to deal with. They aren't going to go away so you must choose plants that can take the abuse such situations present.

Infertile soil can usually be coaxed to a friable growing medium for plants. In the worst cases you may build raised beds and purchase the best soil money can buy to grow your plants in. Most of the soil out there, however, just needs copious amounts of organic matter to bring back the life that bulldozers, heavy equipment and years of neglect have stolen from it. Swampy, water-logged soil is another matter. Here, special work is required to remove the water and dry out the site before plants can grow well. You may choose not to fight the sight and select plants that can grow in boggy situations.

Know the conditions of your yard, then research what plants would do well in that site—right plant, right place. When you know which plants you need, you might keep a list handy in the car. That way when you're tempted to buy, you'll have your list handy to be sure you're buying exactly what the garden needs. I cannot over emphasize that choosing the best plants for your site is the most important step to achieving a healthy, thriving landscape.

Grouping Plants Together

Let's say that you have a very tall townhouse with grey exterior siding. The tall corners of the structure can be softened by placing a pyramidal-shaped plant there. You decide on a Foster holly which has blue-green evergreen foliage and an easily clipped, loosely pyramidal shape. The shape softens the harsh architectural lines of the corner and the dark blue-green foliage complements the grey siding beautifully. It will grow to fit the space you've allotted it nicely and can be lightly clipped to maintain that shape once a year. It's a good plant choice, but don't stop there. By combining other shapes with the holly you will make the picture more interesting and enhance the planting further.

You might combine this holly with the rounded form and unusual color of 'Crimson Pygmy' barberry, a burgundy-leafed shrub. Then to liven the scene some more, you add a ground cover of 'Burgundy Glow' ajuga, a variegated groundcover with green, crimson and cream leaves to cover the bed. The forms complement one another, the colors coordinate with each other and the architecture and the leaf textures go together nicely to round out this low-maintenance combination.

When visualizing groups of plants it helps to roughly sketch their basic forms on paper. It can be as simple as drawing basic shapes to signify plants—a circle fronting a triangle to indicate a pyramidal holly and rounded barberry, with horizontal lines in front to refer to a groundcover.

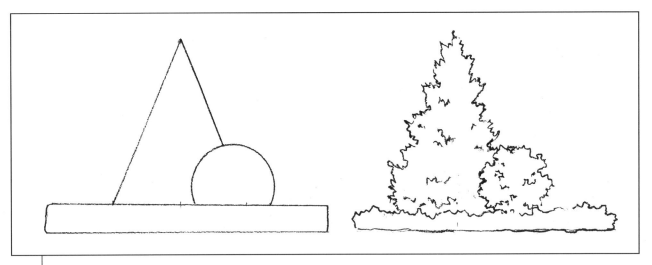

Learn to look at plants as basic shapes and you will be able to combine them effectively and with interest in the landscape.

This helps you visualize how each form relates to the other before you begin digging.

Visualize the garden like you would a room in your house and place the largest plant first. In your living room you'd position the sofa first; in the garden it might be a tree or a group of large shrubs. Move on to place the coffee table and side tables in your living room—this translates to shrubs and "medium" sized plants on your garden plan. Finally you'd place accessories like lamps, magazines, and knickknacks on living room tables. In the garden this would equate to groundcovers or smaller flowering plants. Notice too, that in the living room the number of things increases as the objects get smaller. It's the same in the garden. For a mixed effect, place one tree, three or five medium shaped shrubs, and several dozen groundcovers or pots of annual plants together. The smaller the plant, the more of it must be used to be noticed.

A mistake many gardeners make is to buy one or two small "six-packs" of annuals like pansies which are then planted around the base of the tree in the front yard. The pansies will scarcely be noticed because there are so few of them. Instead, buy several dozen and plant them closer together than the recommended spacing on the nursery tag. In the fall, perhaps you'll interplant the pansies with 25 or 50 tulip bulbs so that the spring show will be equally spectacular. The smaller the plant, the larger the quantity you'll set out for visual impact.

If you're still bent on buying a pack or two of small plants on impulse, plant them in a container close to the front door where they can be appreciated up close. Better yet, group several containers of interesting plants together so that each one complements the others and helps to create a substantial presentation.

Planting in Layers

"Layering" is the term I use to refer to the practice of grouping plants in a unified and pleasing way. All too often we are swept up with the impulse to buy plants that have caught our eye, but by taking the time to analyze how each plant works with its neighbors in the garden, you'll create a pleasing "layered" or "tapestry" effect that is beautiful. Remember, the largest plants should be placed first. In most gardens the largest elements are trees. In the case of the townhouse garden, however, small ornamental trees or large tree-like shrubs will be the largest element. If you're designing a flower border, the largest element will be the most substantial plant—perhaps a butterfly bush. Likewise with container gardens, the largest plant gets placed first.

Using a plan helps to visualize where these key players should go. If you have trouble visualizing from a plan you may construct a small model of the garden and use paper cut-outs of trees and shrubs in differing shapes until you hit upon a pleasing combination. This is much easier than having to move large plants later!

After you've placed the largest elements, move on to place the shrubs and follow these with the smaller plants. Plan for "points of interest" throughout your plan by placing vertical shapes or unusual bursts of color where character and interest is needed. Tall vertical shapes, like that of an ornamental grass, are visually stimulating and draw the focus straight to them. For this reason, don't go overboard in using too many spiky forms. Instead place vertical plants where they will provide points of interest around focal points or features you wish to attract attention to.

Layer plant textures throughout plantings for a rich and lush appearance. This is where foliage plays a key role in the garden. Flowers are transient at best, so foliage must be the first consideration in layering groups of plants. Textures should blend harmoniously together—a large smooth leaf against many smaller grassy leaves, for instance, or lacy fern fronds against the large variegated leaves of a hosta. These combinations of texture create depth and richness in small spaces and can be worked in and around shrubs and other substantial plants beautifully. Bulbs, self-seeding plants like foxgloves, annuals and creeping plants between patio stones all give short bursts of seasonal color and enliven the foliage display even more.

*When creating
a planting plan,
place the largest
plant first,
followed by
medium sized
plants and
graduating down
to the smallest.*

Planting by Color

Luckily, the plant kingdom doesn't present us with just one shade of green—like the one green crayon in the small box of colors. The garden world is more like the big box of crayons. We have apple green, yellow-green, shamrock green, forest green, olive green, pine green, lime green and a host of others. Green isn't the only foliage color either. There are plants that sport leaves of burgundy, grey, cream, silver, and gold; not to mention variegation of cream, white and gold to combine with green plants. There are plants with interesting bark, autumn color, winter texture and colorful berries as well. In fact, flower colors aren't just one shade or another either. In the garden world of color there are thousands, maybe millions, of colors that make up the "color box". There's no such thing as just purple, or yellow or red flowers. Think instead of orchid, violet, blue-violet, gold, lemon, yellow-orange, sunflower, scarlet, apple red, crimson, rosy red, strawberry, watermelon, magenta and mulberry. What a wide spectrum the flower world covers and what a joy it is.

It's important, of course, not to get carried away with too much leaf and flower color in making flower beds and borders. Too much color can be too much of a good thing. Most designers prefer to coordinate borders with two or three colors that are either "warm" like scarlet, gold and orange, or "cool" like grey, rose and blue. Borders improve even more by using an abundance of foliage plants like lamb's ears and ornamental grasses to keep the theme together as flowering plants bloom and change. In more vibrant color schemes of crimson and gold, bright blue or dark purple can be used to tone down and blend colors. Likewise, in pastel schemes, white flowering or variegated plants can be used to blend colors nicely. It helps to punctuate pastel plantings by dropping brighter toned flowering plants among the pastel colors. These act to energize pastel colors and accentuate their coloring. For example, you might try planting a bright pink daylily against pastel pink yarrow to accentuate each plant's texture as well as highlight the pale color of the yarrow.

The color of your townhouse should be of prime consideration in choosing flower colors. Cool colored flowers of blue, white or pale pink look nice next to homes sporting cool colored facades while warm toned flowers of red, orange and gold look best against warm colored facades. If you want cut flowers for the house choose flower colors that complement the interior of your home as well. Often the colors you use in upholstery and drapery fabrics can be worked through the garden for better visual flow from the indoors to the outdoors.

The Best Plants for Townhouse Gardens

Choosing the best plants for your garden depends largely upon the conditions and climate of the area you're gardening in. The following are lists of those plants that do well in the eastern portion of the United States—notably zones two through seven. If you are gardening outside this region, consult local nurseries in your area for plants that perform well in your area. Your county extension service may also provide plant lists and selection advice.

The United States is broken up into different climate zones according to the lowest temperatures reached in the winter. It's important to know your zone so you can choose plants that will not succumb to weather that is too hot or cold. For the most part, reputable local nurseries offer plants that do well in the particular climate they sell in. To be sure, ask your local extension agent or nursery what zone you are gardening in.

Plants for Shady Sites:

Ajuga	(*Ajuga reptans*)
Astilbe	(*Astilbe spp.*)
Aucuba	(*Aucuba japonica*)
Azalea	(*Rhododendron spp.*)
Bleeding Heart	(*Dicentra spp.*)
Cardinal Flower	(*Lobelia cardinalis*)
Coleus	(*Coleus x hybridus*)
Columbine	(*Aquilegia spp.*)
Eastern Redbud	(*Cercis canadensis*)
Epimedium	(*Epimedium spp.*)
Ferns	
Flowering Dogwood	(*Cornus florida*)
Hosta	(*Hosta spp. and hybrids*)
Hydrangea	(*Hydrangea spp.*)
Impatiens	(*Impatiens wallerana*)
Inkberry	(*Ilex glabra*)
Liriope	(*Liriope muscari*)
Moss	
Mountain Laurel	(*Kalmia latifolia*)
Nandina	(*Nandina domestica*)
Pachysandra	(*Pachysandra terminalis*)
Perennial Begonia	(*Begonia grandis*)
Periwinkle	(*Vinca minor*)
Pieris	(*Pieris japonica*)
Pulmonaria	(*Pulmonaria spp.*)
Rhododendron	(*Rhododendron spp.*)
Serviceberry	(*Amalanchier spp.*)
Solomons Seal	(*Polygonatum odoratum*)
Violets	(*Viola spp.*)
Woodland Phlox	(*Phlox divaricata*)

Plants for Sunny Sites:

Ageratum	(*Ageratum houstonianum*)
Alyssum	(*Lobularia maritima*)
Asters	(*Aster spp.*)

Barberry	*(Berberis spp.)*
Blueberry	*(Vaccinium corymbosum)*
Boxwood	*(Buxus sempervirens)*
Burning Bush	*(Euonymous alata)*
Catmint	*(Nepeta spp.)*
Cherry Laurel	*(Prunus laurocerasus)*
Clematis	*(Clematis spp.)*
Coral Bells	*(Heuchera spp.)*
Coreopsis	*(Coreopsis spp.)*
Cotoneaster	*(Cotoneaster spp.)*
Crabapple	*(Malus spp.)*
Crape Myrtle	*(Lagerstroemia hybrids)*
Creeping Phlox	*(Phlox subulata)*
Creeping Thyme	*(Thymus spp.)*
Daylily	*(Hemerocallis spp. and hybrids)*
Dianthus	*(Dianthus spp.)*
Euonymous	*(Euonymous japonica)*
Hawthorn	*(Crataegus spp.)*
Holly	*(Ilex spp.)*
Honeysuckle	*(Lonicera spp.)*
Iris	*(Iris spp.)*
Japanese Maple	*(Acer palmatum)*
Japanese Snowbell	*(Styrax japonicus)*
Juniper	*(Juniperus spp.)*
Lantana	*(Lantana camara)*
Liatris	*(Liatris spicata)*
Lobelia	*(Lobelia erinus)*
Marigold	*(Tagetes spp.)*
Nicotiana	*(Nicotiana spp.)*
Northern Bayberry	*(Myrica pensylvanica)*
Pansy	*(Viola spp.)*
Peony	*(Paeonia spp.)*
Periwinkle	*(Vinca minor)*
Petunia	*(Petunia x hybrida)*
Privet	*(Ligustrum spp.)*
Red-Twig Dogwood	*(Cornus alba)*
Roses	*(Rosa spp.)*
Russian Sage	*(Perovskia atriplicifolia)*
Salvia	*(Salvia spp.)*
Santolina	*(Santolina spp.)*

Sedum   *(Sedum spp.)*
Silverbell   *(Halesia carolina)*
Sunflower   *(Helianthus annuus)*
Sweetbay Magnolia   *(Magnolia virginiana)*
Verbena   *(Verbena peruviana)*
Veronica   *(Veronica spp.)*
Winterberry   *(Ilex verticillata)*
Yew   *(Taxus spp.)*
Zinnia   *(Zinnia elegans)*

Best Small Trees:

Crape Myrtle   *(Lagerstroemia hybrids)*
Eastern Redbud   *(Cercis canadensis)*
Flowering Dogwood   *(Cornus florida)*
Fringe Tree   *(Chionanthus virginicus)*
Japanese Maple   *(Acer palmatum)*
Serviceberry   *(Amelanchier spp.)*
Silverbell   *(Halesia carolina)*
Sourwood   *(Oxydendrum arboreum)*
Stewartia   *(Stewartia spp.)*
Sweetbay Magnolia   *(Magnolia virginiana)*

Best Evergreen Shrubs:

Arborvitae   *(Thuja occidentalis)*
Aucuba   *(Aucuba japonica)*
Boxwood   *(Buxus sempervirens)*
Cherry Laurel   *(Prunus laurocerasus)*
Evergreen Euonymus   *(Euonymus japonica)*
Holly   *(Ilex spp.)*
Inkberry   *(Ilex glabra)*
Nandina   *(Nandina domestica)*
Rhododendron   *(Rhododendron spp.)*
Rosemary   *(Rosmarinus officinalis)*
Yew   *(Taxus spp.)*

Plants for Scent/Fragrance:

Angels Trumpet/Datura	*(Brugmansia spp.)*
Bearded Iris	*(Iris germanica)*
Carolina Allspice	*(Calycanthus floridus)*
Clethra	*(Clethra alnifolia)*
Herbal Geraniums	
Honeysuckle	*(Lonicera spp.)*
Koreanspice Viburnum	*(Viburnum carlesii)*
Lilies	*(Lilium spp.)*
Mockorange	*(Philadelphus spp.)*
Pinkshell Azalea	*(Rhododendron vaseyi)*
Pinxterbloom Azalea	*(Rhododendron nudiflorum)*
Summersweet	*(Clethra alnifolia)*
Swamp Azalea	*(Rhododendron viscosum)*
Sweet Azalea	*(Rhododendron arborescens)*
Witch Hazel	*(Hamamelis spp.)*

Climbing Plants for Sun:

Blue Passion Vine	*(Passiflora caerulea)*
Cardinal Climber	*(Ipomoea x multifida)*
Clematis	*(Clematis spp.)*
Climbing Roses	*(Rosa spp.)*
English Ivy	*(Hedera helix)*
Honeysuckle	*(Lonicera spp.)*
Hyacinth Bean	*(Dolichos Lablab)*
Moonvine	*(Ipomoea alba)*
Morning Glory	*(Ipomoea tricolor)*
Scarlet Runner Bean	*(Phaseolus coccineus)*
Wisteria	*(Wisteria spp.)*

Climbing Plants for Shade:

Climbing Hydrangea	*(H. anomala petiolaris)*
English Ivy	*(Hedera helix)*
Virgin's Bower	*(Clematis virginiana)*
Virginia Creeper	*(Parthenocissus quinquefolia)*

Terrific Foliage Plants:

Astilbe	*(Astible spp.)*
Chives	*(Allium schoenoprasum)*
Coral Bells	*(Heuchera micrantha)*
Ferns	
Hosta	*(Hosta spp. and hybrids)*
Lamb's Ears	*(Stachys byzantina)*
Liriope	*(Liriope muscari)*
Siberian Iris	*(Iris sibirica)*
Solomons Seal	*(Polygonatum odoratum)*
Thyme	*(Thymus spp.)*

Variegated Foliage:

Butterfly Bush	*(Buddleia davidii* 'Harequin'*)*
Caladium	*(Caladium florida hybrids)*
Euonymous	*(Euonymus fortunei)*
Garden Phlox	*(Phlox paniculata* 'Nora Leigh'*)*
Hosta	*(Hosta spp. and hybrids)*
Hydrangea	*(H. macrophylla* 'Mariesii Variegata'*)*
Iris	*(Iris pallida* 'Variegata'*)*
Japanese Painted Fern	*(Athyrium nipponicum* 'Pictum'*)*
Lamium	*(Lamium maculatum)*
Liriope	*(Liriope muscari)*
Ornamental Grasses	
Pulmonaria	*(Pulmonaria saccharata)*
Solomons Seal	*(Polygonatum odoratum)*
Violet	*(Viola* 'Variegata'*)*
Yucca	*(Yucca filamentosa* 'Color Guard'*)*

Plants for Dry Shade:

Aucuba	*(Aucuba japonica)*
Epimedium	*(Epimedium spp.)*
Liriope	*(Liriope muscari)*
Inkberry	*(Ilex glabra)*

Drought Tolerant Plants:

Barberry	*(Berberis spp.)*
Butterfly Weed	*(Asclepias tuberosa)*
Coreopsis	*(Coreopsis spp.)*
Juniper	*(Juniperus spp.)*
Lamb's Ears	*(Stachys byzantina)*
Liatris	*(Liatris spicata)*
Northern Bayberry	*(Myrica pensylvanica)*
Purple Coneflowers	*(Echinacea purpurea)*
Rose Campion	*(Lychnis coronaria)*
Russian Sage	*(Perovskia atriplicifolia)*
Santolina	*(Santolina spp.)*
Sedum	*(Sedum spp.)*
Thyme	*(Thymus spp.)*
Yarrow	*(Achillia spp.)*

Plants for Moist Sites:

Bee Balm	*(Monarda didyma)*
Carolina Allspice	*(Calycanthus floridus)*
Highbush Blueberry	*(Vaccinium corymbosum)*
Inkberry	*(Ilex glabra)*
Iris	*(Iris spp.)*
Lowbush Blueberry	*(Vacciuium angustifolium)*
Red-Twig Dogwood	*(Cornus alba)*
Summersweet	*(Clethra alnifolia)*
Swamp Azalea	*(Rhododendron viscosum)*
Viburnum	*(Viburnum spp.)*

Plants for Water Gardens:

Anacharis	*(Elodea canadensis)*
Cattail	*(Typha latifolia)*
Cambomba	*(Cambomba caroliniana)*
Iris	*(Iris spp.)*
Lotus	*(Nelumbo spp.)*
Pickerel Rush	*(Pontederia cordata)*

Variegated Sweetflag   *(Acorus calamus variegatus)*
Waterlily   *(Nymphaea spp.)*

Plants to Attract Birds:

Barberry   *(Berberis spp.)*
Bayberry   *(Myrica spp.)*
Beautyberry   *(Callicarpa Americana)*
Black-eyed Susan   *(Rudbeckia fulgida)*
Cherry Laurel   *(Prunus laurocerasus)*
Chokecherry   *(Prunus virginiana)*
Coreopsis   *(Coreopsis spp.)*
Cosmos   *(Cosmos bipinnatus)*
Cotoneaster   *(Cotoneaster spp.)*
Crabapple   *(Malus spp.)*
Flowering Dogwood   *(Cornus florida)*
Grape Vines   *(Vitis spp.)*
Highbush Blueberry   *(Vaccinium corymbosum)*
Holly   *(Ilex spp.)*
Inkberry   *(Ilex glabra)*
Juniper   *(Juniperus spp.)*
Liatris   *(Liatris spp.)*
Lowbush Blueberry   *(Vaccinium angustifolium)*
Purple Coneflower   *(Echinacea purpurea)*
Pyracantha   *(Pyracantha spp.)*
Rugosa Rose   *(Rosa rugosa)*
Serviceberry   *(Amelanchier spp.)*
Spicebush   *(Lindera benzoin)*
Sunflower   *(Helianthus spp.)*
Switchgrass   *(Panicum virgatum)*
Viburnum   *(Viburnum spp.)*
Winterberry   *(Ilex verticillata)*
Zinnia   *(Zinnia elegans)*

Plants to Attract Butterflies:

Asters   *(Aster spp.)*
Beauty Bush   *(Kolkwitzia amabilis)*

Bee Balm	(*Monarda didyma*)
Black-eyed Susan	(*Rudbeckia fulgida*)
Butterfly Bush	(*Buddleia davidii*)
Butterfly Weed	(*Asclepias tuberosa*)
Catmint	(*Nepeta spp.*)
Coreopsis	(*Coreopsis spp.*)
Flowering Dogwood	(*Cornus florida*)
Fruit Trees	
Fennel	(*Foeniculum vulgare*)
Heliotrope	(*Heliotropium arborescens*)
Joe-pye Weed	(*Eupatorium spp.*)
Lavender	(*Lavandula spp.*)
Lilac	(*Syringa spp.*)
Marigold	(*Tagetes spp.*)
Parsley	(*Petroselinum crispum*)
Purple Coneflower	(*Echinacea purpurea*)
Redbud	(*Cercis canadensis*)
Sedum	(*Sedum spp.*)
Spicebush	(*Lindera benzoin*)
Thyme	(*Thymus spp.*)
Tithonia	(*Tithonia rotundifolia*)
Viburnum	(*Viburnum spp.*)
Violets	(*Viola spp.*)
Yarrow	(*Achillea spp.*)
Zinnia	(*Zinnia spp.*)

Plants to Attract Hummingbirds:

Bee Balm	(*Monarda didyma*)
Butterfly Bush	(*Buddleia spp.*)
Cardinal Climber	(*Ipomoea x multifida*)
Cardinal Flower	(*Lobelia cardinalis*)
Columbine	(*Aquilegia canadensis*)
Coral Bells	(*Heuchera sanguinea*)
Foxglove	(*Digitalis purpurea*)
Honeysuckle	(*Lonicera spp.*)
Lilac	(*Syringa spp.*)
Lilies	(*Lilium spp.*)
Penstemon	(*Penstemon spp.*)

Petunia	*(Petunia x hybrida)*
Red-hot Poker	*(Kniphofia uvaria)*
Scarlet Salvia	*(Salvia splendens)*
Scarlet Runner Bean	*(Phaseolus coccineus)*
Trumpet Honeysuckle	*(Lonicera sempervirens)*
Trumpet Vine	*(Campsis radicans)*
Weigela	*(Weigela Florida)*

Groundcovers for Sun:

Creeping Cotoneaster	*(Cotoneaster adpressus)*
Creeping Phlox	*(Phlox subulata)*
Creeping Thyme	*(Thymus serpyllum)*
Lamb's Ears	*(Stachys byzantina)*
Periwinkle	*(Vinca minor)*
Sedum	*(Sedum spp.)*
Spreading Junipers	*(Juniperus spp.)*

Groundcovers for Shade:

Ajuga	*(Ajuga reptans)*
Foamflower	*(Tiarella cordifolia)*
Lily-of-the-valley	*(Convallaria majalis)*
Lirope	*(Liriope muscari)*
Mondo Grass	*(Ophiopogon japonicus)*
Pachysandra	*(Pachysandra terminalis)*
Pulmonaria	*(Pulmonaria saccharata)*
Scotch Moss	*(Sagina subulata 'Aurea')*
Spotted Dead Nettle	*(Lamium maculatum)*
Sweet Woodruff	*(Galium odoratum)*
Winter Creeper	*(Euonymus fortunei)*

Plants for Winter Interest:

Aucuba	*(Aucuba japonica)*
Autumn Fern	*(Dryopteris erythrosora)*
Blueberry	*(Vaccinium spp.)*
Eastern Red Cedar	*(Juniperus virginiana)*

Holly	(*Ilex spp.*)
Lauder's Walkingstick	(*Corylus avellana* 'Contorta')
Lenten Rose	(*Helleborus spp.*)
Mahonia	(*Mahonia spp.*)
Ornamental Grasses	
Red-twig Dogwood	(*Cornus alba*)
River Birch	(*Betula nigra* 'Heritage')
Rugosa Rose	(*Rosa Rugosa*)
Winterberry	(*Ilex verticillata*)
Witch Hazel	(*Hamamelis x intermedia*)

Plants for Between Pavers and Stones:

Alyssum	(*Lobularia maritima*)
Ajuga	(*Ajuga reptans*)
Creeping Jenny	(*Lysimachia nummularia*)
Hen and Chicks	(*Sempervivum spp.*)
Mazus	(*Mazus reptans*)
Moss Sandwort	(*Arenaria subulata*)
Sea Thrift	(*Armeria setacea*)
Sedum	(*Sedum spp.*)
Thyme	(*Thymus spp.*)

Dwarf Shrubs for Townhouse Gardens:

Abelia, 'Edward Goucher'
Arborvitae, 'Hetzi Midget', 'Little Gem', 'Tiny Tim'
Azalea, 'Gable Hybrids', 'Kurume Hybrids', 'Satsuki Hybrids'
Barberry, 'Crimson Pygmy'
Boxwood, English, Korean and Wintergreen
Cherry Laurel, 'Otto Luyken'
Cotoneaster, 'Tom Thumb'
Dwarf Nandina, 'Harbour Dwarf'
Holly, 'Blue Angel', 'China Boy', 'China Girl', 'Chinese Dwarf',
    'Convexa', 'Helleri', 'Petite Point', 'Shamrock'
Hydrangea, 'A.G. Annabelle'
Juniper, 'Blue Star', 'Blue Point', 'Grey Gleam', 'Moonglow',
'Robusta Green', 'Skyrocket', 'Spartan', 'Gold Star'

Leucothoe, 'Scarletta'
Mugo Pine
Rhododendron, 'PJM', 'Yaku Princess'
Winterberry,'Red Sprite'
Yew, 'Hicks', 'Dwarf English'

TOWNHOUSE TIP

To plant a great garden in a minimum of time you should plant thickly in the beginning and be prepared to thin plantings later. Plant fast-growing climbers like morning glories to fill in until slow growers like clematis can catch up. For the first couple of years you may fill in gaps with colorful annuals or even vegetables or herbs and tuck spring blooming bulbs among plantings. Groundcovers always lend a finished look quicker when closely planted initially. You may also use large leafed plants like hosta and elephant ears to take up space while trees and shrubs mature. Group lushly planted containers with ornaments for interest on the patio and rely on lots of structure like arches and trellises for vertical interest.

7.

Container Gardens

One of the most lamentable scenes to me is a row of townhouses, each with the same deck at the back—and each deck empty and bare of beauty. How useful and wonderful they would be with pretty furniture and lushly planted pots of pretty flowers! The deck, like the patio, is an outdoor extension of the house. Lovely furnishings make the space livable, and containers filled with thriving plants soften the transition from the inside to the outside like nothing else can.

If you're living two stories up with a deck, the only way you'll be able to grow plants is in containers. Container gardening is quite different from growing plants in cultivated ground. Because they are out of the moist ground and their pots dry out quickly, container grown plants require more frequent watering and care. Yet, container gardens pay back the effort with their beautiful contribution to the garden. Also, they can be changed inexpensively and moved around on a whim.

Contained plants are just that—they're contained or housed in decorative pots, window boxes, baskets, wire racks, wooden boxes or anything that can hold a bit of soil and a plant. Some enthusiastic container gardeners plant in cans, old boots, bird cages, hats, pots and pans, crockery—anything unusual and interesting serves.

Almost any plant can be grown in a container. There's something almost romantic about a large pot overflowing with healthy flowering plants in many textures and pleasing colors. Small trees and shrubs too, can be grown successfully in containers. One advantage to growing some of your plants in containers is that potted plants soften the hardscape of deck and patio areas. They enable you to keep a constantly changing array of seasonal color on the patio for visual interest. Containers dress up plain patio or deck areas and are great for enhancing and marking the entry of a home, as well as directing traffic flow in the garden. They make it possible to grow exotic plants outside for the summer and enable us to move tender plants inside for the winter. Container plantings can be used to create vertical interest, to introduce different materials to the landscape and to draw butterflies and hummingbirds to the deck. They enable children to participate in gardening and make it possible for less active gardeners to have a few plants to tend without all the bending ground-level gardens require. You can even use containers to introduce a bit of water to the garden.

Gardens Contained

Plants grown in containers are elevated to the status of "decoration". Because they are commonly removed from the garden and placed in high-traffic areas they are more special. Most often container gardens are displayed in significant locations such as at the sides of a doorway. The idea is to place them anywhere they can be appreciated up close. Walls, for example, lend themselves to container culture when hung with baskets or "wall racks" suitable for displaying seasonal plants. Used en masse, these displays create an artistic effect on even the most mundane of vertical surfaces, which also makes them easily accessible for daily care.

Selecting Containers

Containers such as terra cotta pots, hanging baskets, window boxes, deck railing boxes or collections of pots grouped along porch steps offer an easy way to garden. Continuity is a beautiful thing and when planting an entire group of pots it's wise to use the same color scheme for all the pots. In my own garden I have six large terra cotta pots on the brick patio. Each spring the six are planted with the same palette of plants. The combinations are changed from year to year—one year it may be fragrant lilies with purple and white alyssum cascading down the sides of the pots, another year it may be a mix of hot colored flowers. I favor large containers planted so that they overflow and the container is almost hidden.

Because they are positioned to be seen up close, the containers that hold your plants should be chosen with care. Consider how they will coordinate with other materials in the garden and how they will convey the "theme" or feeling you wish to impart. Casual, country cottage gardens benefit from the classic good looks of terra cotta pots, while formal boxwood parterres call for white Chippendale-styled boxes or dark Grecian-styled urns. The color and type of material the container consists of also influence the selection of plants grown in it. It all flows back to the design intent of the garden. Your design focus, whether formal or informal, should influence every selection you make.

Natural containers of wood, stone and terra cotta look best in most gardens. However, terra cotta colored fiberglass or heavy-duty plastic is a better buy in areas where freezing winter weather destroys natural clay containers. Manufacturers now offer many quality designs in plastic and fiberglass and when lushly planted, they can be hard to tell apart from the real materials they imitate.

Remember the importance of scale when choosing containers for your garden. Most gardeners choose planters that are out of scale to the site they are decorating. Larger containers of 18- or 24-inch diameter, for example, will appear more substantial and in scale on large decks and patios. Masses of plants always look great, so group similar types of pots together in a variety of sizes for a cohesive effect.

Choosing Plants for Container Gardens

The joy of container gardening is that there's no right or wrong way to combine plants. The combinations of plants possible for any given garden container are endless. It helps to experiment by placing various plants together in the nursery to see how they look before you settle on the combination that works for you. Attention to the details of color coordination, plant texture and massed groupings will provide interest and complexity to your desktop garden efforts.

Late every spring I look forward to changing the tired looking pansies in the six large terra cotta pots on our brick patio. I take great pains to select the right plants for the long summer season since I know I'll be looking at them for a long time. The plants that grace these pots are the focal point of the patio area and must always be presentable for entertaining throughout the summer.

Containers are great for seasonal bursts of color on the deck or patio. To keep them interesting and healthy looking, plants should be changed three times a year beginning with blooming spring bulbs (planted in the fall) and followed with flowering annuals for the summer and evergreen shrubs or pansies for autumn and winter. Ivy, thyme, vinca vine, creeping phlox and other evergreen trailers can be planted at the edges of pots to trail down the side and create year-round interest for more permanent plantings as well. Summer annuals like begonias, petunias, geraniums and marigolds are most commonly chosen for container gardens, but there are other plants that do well in them too.

Evergreen shrubs, perennials, ornamental grasses, fruits, vegetables, water gardens and even small trees can be showcased in containers on the deck or patio. Almost any plant that can be grown in the ground can be grown in a container, but while seasonal plants like annuals withstand a lot of crowding, larger specimens cannot. You'll have to select a pot with plenty of growing room and offer some protection from drying winter winds and freezing temperatures in order to keep large woody specimens alive.

Another consideration when selecting plants for your containers is to plant for longevity. "Overplant" spring flowering bulbs with frost-hardy pansies in the fall for longer displays. Early bulbs can also be interplanted with later flowering bulbs for a longer floral display instead of the few days of glory most bulbs provide.

Plant spring flowering bulbs under cool-weather loving pansies for a beautiful, long-blooming spring show.

When grouping plants, take care to choose plants that look good together and combine them well with the material of the container. It's here that a certain amount of artistry takes over. Planting containers is subjective. No two people combine plants in the same manner and because of this you're allowed a bit of artistic license. Even in planting containers, however, it's best to choose the right plant for the right place. Note the sun conditions of the place where pots sit throughout the seasons and select plants accordingly. Sun loving plants should go together in sun-bound pots and shade lovers should be combined together for shady spots around the garden.

Container Planting How-to

Maintaining healthy container gardens is easy when you start with the proper growing medium. Most container gardens benefit from a good potting mix that has a light texture. These "potting mixes" don't dry to the clay-like hardness of ordinary top soil and are lighter than regular garden soil when wet—an important factor for hanging baskets and window boxes. Because lightweight potting mixes are rich in perlite too, roots have an easier time expanding and reaching their full potential.

Soil specifically suited to container gardens is loose and airy and contains lots of organic matter and some sharp sand for adequate drainage. The potting mix you choose shouldn't be too heavy in consistency. Look for mixes that contain perlite, vermiculite, peat or other lightweight growing mediums. Very light soil mixes should be combined with screened compost or shredded leaves to increase fertility and moisture retention. Heavier soils can also be made lighter with tiny bark "fines", screened compost, shredded leaves or potting soil.

If you don't want to be a slave to daily watering during the summer, use a water saving polymer like "Moisture Miser" as a soil additive before you pot up container plants. These crystals become gelatin-like when plumped with water and help prevent excessive dryness in container plantings.

Before filling a container, you should cover the hole at the bottom with a small square of screen mesh, a layer of gravel or a shard of pottery to prevent loss of the potting medium. These barriers allow sufficient drainage of excess water without loss of the potting soil. If your pot doesn't have a hole in the bottom, pot up plants in a plain plastic garden pot with drainage holes. This can be lifted out of the decorative pot for watering.

Because you're creating an artificial environment of sorts, seasonal plants will be able to stand more crowded growing conditions than if they were planted in the ground, so pack them in till they seem to overflow the pot. This is one instance where you can safely disregard the rules of plant spacing. Containers should be made to look like they are alive with an abundance of plants and plants should obscure the container.

Great Container Garden Combinations

The combinations of plants that you could use in container gardens is limited only by your imagination. Here are a few of my favorite planting combinations that may inspire your efforts:

— Terra cotta pots with red begonia, dusty miller, white petunias, red miniature roses and green ivy spilling over the sides. (Sun)

— White window boxes with red geraniums, variegated vinca vine and silver-edged creeping thyme spilling over the front. (Sun)

— White Chippendale-styled planter boxes filled with pink geraniums, dusty miller, white petunias, pink begonias, purple ageratum and white alyssum. (Sun)

— Terra cotta pots planted in an all-white theme with white nicotiana, petunias, alyssum and miniature roses. (Sun)

— Terra cotta pots filled with herbs such as thyme, chives, parsley, oregano, dill and the small woodland strawberry, Fraises de Bois. (Sun)

— Hanging baskets of pink verbena, white petunias, variegated ivy and red ivy geraniums. (Sun)

— Dark green Chippendale-styled boxes with rose trees underplanted with masses of begonias, lobelia, petunias, thyme or alyssum. (Sun)

— Terra cotta pots with green and white veined caladiums underplanted with variegated winter creeper and silver edged thyme. (Shade)

— Deck railing boxes planted with spring blooming bulbs such as daffodils, grape hyacinth, tulips and crocus, with pansies filling in. (Sun)

— A wooden carpenter's box planted with yellow daffodils and interplanted with forget-me-nots. (Sun or shade)

— A contemporary concrete bowl planted with assorted colors of pansies in shades of purple, blue, white and pale yellow. (Sun or shade)

— A half whiskey barrel filled with varieties of ivy geranium in pink, burgundy and white. (Sun)

— A patriotic garden in a white Chippendale-styled planter box with red geraniums, white petunias and blue lobelia. (Sun)

— A hanging foliage garden made up of asparagus ferns, ivy, creeping dusty miller, vinca vine and creeping thyme. (Sun)

— Terra cotta bowls of multicolored impatiens surrounded by pink polka dot plants. (Shade)

— A kid's "Pizza Garden" in a half whiskey barrel consisting of all the plants needed to make a pizza: a tomato plant, oregano, basil and parsley. (Sun)

— Window boxes with morning glories and moon vines trained up strings to form a flowering screen. (Sun)

— Large terra cotta pots with hoops of red cardinal climber, orange and yellow Asiatic lilies, red dianthus, creeping thyme and blue salvia. (Sun)

— Tall dracaena plants underplanted with cascading ferns in a matched pair of stone planters. (Shade)

— A large "herb bowl" planted with parsley, thyme, sage, oregano, chives and edible flowers. (Sun)

— An extra large terra cotta-like fiberglass container planted as a water garden with waterlilies, submerged plants, cattails and a few goldfish. (Sun)

— Large hibiscus trees underplanted with begonias, alyssum and impatiens in a large Chippendale box. (Sun)

— Terra cotta pots with red begonia, dusty miller, white petunias, a red miniature rose bush and green ivy spilling over the sides. (Sun)

— Twin lollypop-shaped herbal geranium trees in terra cotta pots underplanted with lilac alyssum. (Sun)

— Terra cotta pots with "tepees" fashioned from bamboo poles where vining plants like morning glory, cardinal climber, ivy or love-in-a-puff are trained and underplanted with a carpet of alyssum. (Sun)

Maintenance

Because container plantings are always on view and exposed to a wide variety of climatic changes, regular care will be a necessity. Daily watering is a must in sultry summer weather as plants grown in containers tend to dry out faster and leach away valuable fertilizer faster than plants grown in the ground. For this reason a weak solution of water soluble fertilizer can be applied with daily waterings or in heavier weekly feedings. Because container gardens are always on display, spent blossoms should be removed regularly to keep plants looking their best as well. All this can be accomplished in a few minutes after work or in the morning.

A terrace or patio never looks finished until it's softened with plants. There's something very satisfying about seeing big pots overflowing with healthy plants in many textures and pleasing colors. With a bit of imagination and daily maintenance your container plantings will reward you with many seasons of beauty.

TOWNHOUSE TIP

You can create the ambiance of a mature garden faster with substantial structures like pergolas, pillars or columns. Even something as simple as a metal arch clothed in annual vines will convey a lush atmosphere. Display art and objects on pillars or on walls, and all you need to complete the picture are plenty of new plantings .

8.

Water in the Garden

No single item will give you more pleasure than a bit of water in the garden. Water is magical. It can create a sense of calm in a hurried world, give the illusion of greater space, "cool" hot locations by visual association, create unusual effects and soothe away harsh surrounding noises—a plus in crowded living spaces. We seem to associate peacefulness and calm with water's smooth stillness. In larger landscapes where water features must be more expansive to be in scale, the element of water can be labor intensive to install. It's much easier to bring the element of water to tiny gardens, however, and with great effect. Small water features are also easy to come by, most being possible to install in a weekend or two.

Having a water garden in the townhouse landscape enables you to grow water-loving plants. Water lilies, lotus, water iris and other "marginal" plants thrive when submerged in water and add a lovely note to the garden design. Another important benefit of water is the wildlife it attracts. Water is more important than food to visiting birds and wild creatures in areas without natural ponds or waterways. In a housing development of hundreds of townhouses, even a small dish of water is seen as an oasis to the birds. Soon after installing a birdbath or tiny garden pond you'll see many creatures that were previously elusive. Wildlife like birds, frogs, turtles, toads and hummingbirds all make the gardening experience richer and tell us that what we are doing is right. After all, the land you occupy began as their home.

Bringing Water to the Townhouse Garden

Water gardening has seen a renaissance of late and its paraphernalia has literally "flooded" the market. It's now possible to have your water any way you like it. You can install a garden pond by digging an impression and lining it with a special rubber liner. Or you can place a recirculating birdbath among the flowers, or hang a wall-mounted fountain on the fence. Small table-top fountains work magic when placed strategically in gardens where they can be both seen and heard. You might sink a whiskey barrel into the ground or plug the hole of a large flower pot and sink it to its rim, then fill it with water, add a waterlily and a couple of small goldfish and have a perfectly respectable water feature for your townhouse garden.

Henry Mitchell, the late garden writer for *The Washington Post*, used to write of creating water gardens out of horse watering troughs. He delighted in facing the plain metal sides with decorative tiles and planting their edges so heavily that visitors scarcely knew they were admiring an implement designed for watering livestock! The possibilities are endless.

Because water is such an attractive feature, however, one word of caution is necessary. In households where small children reside, water should be no more than two inches deep. Deeper water is dangerous to curious children. So play it safe and install a birdbath, wall fountain, Oriental water flute, shallow decorative bowl or a "splash" fountain where water recirculates over rocks.

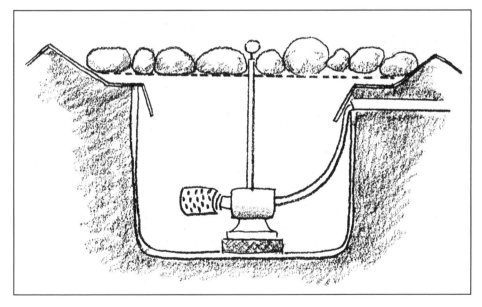

A splash fountain underground reservoir, protected by a safety grate and topped with decorative stones, houses a pump that recirculates splashing water over the rocks. This small, easy-to-install water element is the ideal decorative element for many small gardens.

Placing the Water Feature in the Design

Because it is such an interesting part of the landscape, you'll want to place the water feature where it can be appreciated up close. Water garners a lot of interest, so you'll want to situate the water element on or very near the patio for easy viewing. Nobody should have to trample plants to get a closer look. Also, because water features require a certain amount of maintenance, they need to be placed where they can be accessed for filling and maintenance.

The design of your water garden must, again, repeat the style you have in mind. Formal gardens are not great hosts to attempts as natural waterfalls or wilderness ponds. These are nice, but not believable in formal atmospheres. At best, majestic waterfalls belong in purely informal gardens. In formal gardens a gentle circle or oval reflecting pool may be more believable.

Townhouse developments may once have been wide open natural spaces, but now that space is home to something else. The small areas that make up each individual landscape naturally lend themselves to a more tailored look and it's entirely okay for the water feature to be "obvious"—in a tank, decorative bowl or ornamental pot.

In formal gardens, a free standing fountain may be placed in the center for just the right ornamentation and proper visual effect. An Oriental-inspired garden might benefit from a simple bamboo "water flute", a reed of bamboo that water continually flows through to a small water basin below. Conversely, an informal cottage garden might play host to a decorative wall fountain, or tiny naturalized recirculating fountain for the birds that's surrounded by lush plantings of ferns and other moisture lovers.

Maintaining Water Gardens

The maintenance of your water garden depends upon its complexity. Ponds with fish and plants require a small amount of effort in trimming water lily leaves, feeding plants and fish, topping off the water level and grooming plants around the water's edge. Small water features like birdbaths, table fountains and the like will benefit from regular water changes and an occasional scrubbing with a soft brush to eliminate algae.

If you want fish, and a couple of fish always enliven a water garden, be prepared to bring them into the house for the winter, or to install a "de-icer" that keeps a hole open in the pond for oxygen. This simple device can be found at nurseries that specialize in water gardening. The de-icer is plugged into a grounded outdoor outlet and is thermostatically controlled, coming on only when water temperatures sink below freezing.

To keep the water clear make sure that 70% of the water's surface is covered with foliage—like that from water lily leaves or floating plants. It also helps to keep the water clear if you don't overfeed fish. Do grow submerged plants like anacharis or cambomba that filter sediment naturally and skim any floating debris from the water surface daily.

Water lilies and other submerged plants should be planted in lily baskets in heavy clay soil from your garden, not lightweight "potting soil" that comes in bags from the nursery. Finish planting the water lily by pushing a fertilizer tablet into the clay and topping it all off with an inch of gravel so fish won't muddy the water. Fertilizer tablets for water plants can be found at any nursery that specializes in water gardening (see Sources). Water lilies and lotus are heavy feeders, so be prepared to feed them monthly during the summer growing season for lush growth and flower production.

Fish in the Water Garden

Use discretion when stocking your water garden with fish. Lovely Japanese Koi require the equivalent of a large outdoor aquarium, complete with expensive filtration equipment. Koi typically grow very large and will muddy the water in their restless search for food. For small outdoor water gardens, consider goldfish from the pet store. We currently own a large water garden that holds over 2000 gallons of water. Knowing that they can reach ten inches in length or more, we stocked it with only eight goldfish that were just a few inches long in the beginning. They've since grown to over six inches in length and have populated the pool with many healthy babies. Three years later the balance is maintained because we didn't overstock the pool in the beginning. The number of "fish inches" you stock in your water garden is important because fish waste can upset the balance and foul the water. Less is more—no more than one inch of fish for every ten gallons of water.

TOWNHOUSE TIP

Water gardening has spun off from the landscape industry so that there are actually companies that do nothing but install water gardens. There are even Web sites on the Internet for water gardening aficionados as well as numerous books on the subject. An excellent starting guide for beginners is the Lilypons Water Gardens catalog (see Sources). Lilypons has led the nation in its quest for water in the garden and offers reputable advice. Filled with plants, books, liners and even fish, the catalog is a true inspiration for anyone who longs for the sanctuary of water in the garden.

9.
Furnishings and Accessories

Like the interiors of our homes, outdoor rooms benefit from the addition of furniture and ornamentation. So far, we've discussed the floor of the garden, the structures, ceiling and plantings, but what about a place to sit and reflect when the work is done? When it comes to comfort and relaxation most people look to their own backyards and gardens. You should feel comfortable and be able to relax in your garden retreat. Cheap furniture bought on sale at the drugstore will not be comfortable or durable and won't give the garden the distinction it deserves. Garden furnishings and ornaments should be chosen with as much thought as you would give to furnishing a room inside the house.

When deciding how to furnish your patio or deck it helps to envision it as a room. It may be hard to envision a lush, private enclave when all you've got is a bare, bulldozed lot, but careful thought about the garden you hope to achieve can avert purchasing errors. Many new gardeners mistakenly buy furniture and ornaments that clash with the style of the house and garden. For continuity, consider the style you're comfortable with inside your house. Outdoor furnishings should complement the exterior style of your home as well. A country Victorian house dripping with white gingerbread scrollwork calls for elegant wicker pieces on the porch and heavy antique white iron in the garden. Large estate homes with formal gardens may call for teak English garden benches or dark green neoclassic iron furniture. A rustic cottage retreat calls for bent willow "twig" furniture or Adirondack chairs, a hammock and so forth.

"Theme" based furniture has become trendy lately. It's now possible to create the ambiance of the southwest, English cottage, Italian renaissance, Caribbean or the French countryside. Remember that those cute yellow chairs in the shape of sunflowers may be adorable this season but they'll be passé by next year. Fabrics can also help enhance the mood you're trying to create in the garden. Dark stripes, rich plaids and traditional florals complement formal garden environments while bright stripes and colorful florals create a casual atmosphere.

Before you buy, take measurements of the sitting areas and note what furniture you'll need. You can't go wrong with a sketch of the area on graph paper to help you once you get to the store. Though a dining table and chairs are overwhelmingly the most popular pieces of furniture for gardens, larger outdoor rooms can benefit from intimate seating areas with a couple of comfortable chairs and a settee as well. Be sure to allow for adequate room around each piece. Nobody likes to feel crowded. A simple cafe table and two chairs might be much more intimate and enjoyable on a small terrace than a 60-inch table and four chairs.

Given enough space you may consider a separate seating group in addition to the dining table. With a large number of guests the dining table can be used as a buffet area and extra chairs situated in groups around the garden. Last but not least, give attention to the little "extras" that make the outdoor room special. Market umbrellas, sun shades, planters, outdoor lighting, serving carts, outdoor dinnerware, garden swings, colorful pillows and beautiful sculpture will enhance the space season after season.

Garden Art and Adornment

Many gardeners consider themselves artists and many artists are gardeners; the two go together naturally. Throughout the ages sculpture, fountains, bas reliefs and even paintings have been displayed outdoors. From elaborate Parisian avenues where statues are displayed on pedestals to the simplicity of a terra cotta cat peering out from under the flowers in an English cottage garden, sculpture, art and tasteful garden accessories have always moved to the outdoors in style.

Townhouse gardens will benefit from a focal point or two in the landscape, and though many plant purists eschew garden art as too contrived, tasteful sculpture and artwork can provide a key element in the design process. I'm often impressed by how well artwork integrates into the garden when displayed by savvy garden artisans. Once I saw a subtle urn with the face of a lion at the edge of a small garden pool. Another time, in the heart of the city, I found a copper goddess gracing a small reflecting pool. Each piece of sculpture was beautiful, well placed and reflected the taste of the gardener.

In large public sculpture gardens the flowers are few. Some purists consider art in the garden a horrid detraction from the plants themselves, and there's a very fine line between providing the garden with a few subdued accents and killing the whole picture with a lot of meaningless stuff. Strive to strike a happy medium with sculpture by using art where it will be most appreciated. There are many ways to display art in the garden. You may use a decorative urn or sculpture at the end of a long view or as a focal point at the center of your garden. Walls can often be put into service for gallery displays, as can niches in hedges. Flower beds and borders accept decorative pieces nicely and entries to the house are often great places for a pair of decorative containers.

Traditionally animals, children, military heros, religious figures and mythological characters have figured prominently in garden art. To integrate any piece you're considering you must take into account its scale, placement and harmonious relationship to the surrounding landscape. The piece should fit with the garden style, not be a jarring intrusion to the senses. In tiny gardens consider "framing" the piece with greenery, perhaps in a niche carved into a hedge of yew.

Hand crafted bronze sculptures aren't inexpensive. For years I've personally lamented the fact that the only art I seem to be able to afford is not what I want for my garden. Those gardeners who have more taste than cash should consider topiary, bird houses, decorative stepping stones or elaborate urns as a source of tasteful garden art. Water too can be very sculptural and changeable. Consider the mirror-like quality of still water or the quickened pace of dancing fountains. Even materials garnered from nature lend a sculptural quality to the garden. The ancient Chinese often used rocks in the shape of animals to symbolize the natural world around their gardens. Even something as simple as a piece of driftwood can be elevated to the status of ornament in the right garden environment.

It's a shame that we don't have more sources for affordable garden art in this country. But I'd take even a small exquisite piece of bronze, placed strategically in the garden any day over all the cheap plastic in the world. There are numerous concrete castings of animals, figures, urns and other forms that can grace a new garden inexpensively. To avoid a cluttered look, it's best never to have more than one ornament or focal point on display at one time. To integrate these pieces into the garden place them so that they are partially obscured by foliage. Smaller pieces can be raised on decorative pillars or even a stack of bricks that a vine has been allowed to clamber over. The key is to integrate the piece into the garden. It should come as a pleasant surprise sheltered in the foliage, not be so obvious as to draw attention away from the surroundings. Older concrete pieces are a real find at antique shops, but plain white concrete can be aged with moss so it isn't so bold. Moss, mixed with buttermilk and stirred in a blender, can be painted on concrete statuary to grow and make the piece seem timeworn.

Lighting

Obviously the manner in which you display your artwork is very important, but I would also rate night illumination as a priority for enjoying key pieces. Lighting is relatively inexpensive for the return it gives to the garden. In small spaces consider one accent lamp to highlight a tree or wash over a wall instead of the bare bulb outside the patio door. You may also select several points of interest such as a piece of art, the water garden, a pot or a striking plant to be lit by landscape lighting as well. Don't discount the ambiance of candlelight either. Lanterns, candles, strings of fairy-lights and torches all create inexpensive nighttime atmosphere and give us a reason to turn off the glaring porch light.

Night lighting extends the enjoyment of the garden, especially for those who don't arrive home until after sundown. Garden lights add another dimension to the space, and when installed well, create an environment for entertaining as well. One of the most enchanting gardens I've ever visited was lit at night by a string of tiny Christmas lights strung from a tree at the edge of the terrace. These small white lights enhanced the surroundings nicely and would be easy to string around any garden.

TOWNHOUSE TIP

Trees make beautiful focal points when space is provided for them in the patio design. Consider creating a space for trees to grow through at the middle of the patio or deck for additional shade and interest. Small trees like redbuds and Japanese maples can be limbed up to create a living canopy to the patio area below. Multi-trunk trees like crape myrtle, birch and Japanese snowbell are also beautiful when integrated into the hardscape of outdoor living areas. String tiny white lights throughout their branches for special nighttime atmosphere.

10.
Groundwork and Maintenance

Garden plants require ideal growing conditions to stay healthy. You cannot merely dig holes and plunk plants into the ground and expect the garden to flourish. If you did, you'd literally be burying your money. Plants cannot grow lush if the soil isn't healthy. Every green leaf you see above ground is an indicator of what's happening below ground. It's a lot like our own bodies. We can't see our lungs and hearts but we know they're there; and if we're smart, we do our best to ensure their health. Plants must first be nurtured from underground with organically rich, well drained, airy soil.

What Type of Soil Are You Dealing With?

Begin by taking a look at the soil you have. Dig a small amount of it and ball it up in your hand. Does it stay clumped up? Chances are, you're dealing with soil that's clay based. If the soil falls away and cannot stay clumped together, you're probably dealing with sandy soil. Look at the soil closely. Is it red, sand colored or rich dark brown? Does the texture feel like clay or sand? You can tell a lot just by examining a handful of earth from your garden.

You'll also want to gauge the drainage capacity of the soil in your garden. To do this, dig a small hole and slowly fill it with water. Does the soil drain immediately through the sandy consistency? Or does the water drain very slowly as if it were in clay? Perhaps the water doesn't drain at all, an indication of very heavy clay soil. Knowing the consistency of your soil will help in selecting the types of plants you'll be able to grow in your garden. Some plants like bayberry love sandy soils while azaleas and rhododendrons need acidic, clay-based soil to thrive.

Generally speaking, clay soil holds too much water and bakes to the consistency of concrete when dry, while sandy soils drain so fast they are incapable of holding sufficient moisture for good plant growth. When preparing the soil for planting, you'll need to break up clay for better drainage and enrich sand for better moisture retention. Some county extension agencies analyze soil samples for those interested in more precise soil nutrition.

From "Dirt" to Soil

All soils benefit from "conditioning" by working in generous amounts of organic material before plants go in the ground. When I had my first townhouse garden, the books I consulted were filled with advice on how to prepare the soil. All the English books recommended I "double dig" the soil to a depth of 24 inches, and all the "experts" I consulted told me to add bags of expensive top soil and peat moss.

I soon came to realize that double digging was somebody's idea of a joke. My shovel barely scraped the ground, much less penetrated the concrete-like stuff the weeds and grass grew in. I considered it a true miracle that grass could grow in such lifeless "dirt". Later, I also found out how costly all those bags of "amendments" really are—for my budget, and for the environment. You see, all that peat moss has to come from somewhere, and I learned that it comes from peat bogs which are environmentally sensitive areas that don't recover from "harvesting" for many years. I not only had terrible soil, but I bore the guilt of assaulting the environment in addition! So what's a gardener to do? The answer lies in working smarter, not harder. After nearly winding up in traction from weekends of "soil preparation", I began to do a little research. Surely there were gardeners out there who had perfectly respectable gardens without having to dig down 24 inches and crumble every clod of soil. Careful research proved me correct.

I found that there are basically three ways to prepare beds for planting—digging down, building raised planting beds from rock or timbers and mounding up. Digging down involves the back-breaking labor of double digging and was quickly stricken from the list. Raised beds are actually large "container" gardens constructed from stone, brick, timber or any other material that can be fashioned into a bed to hold soil. Mounded beds are a hybrid of the two—slightly raised, partially dug beds that don't require a wall of expensive material around them, and don't require a lot of deep digging.

The Newspaper and Mulch Method

With further research I unearthed a terrific method for preparing the ground without backaches and expensive soil amendments. I found this method in an article in *Fine Gardening* magazine that told how to use newspapers for making new garden beds. It seemed like a gimmick at first, but I decided to give it a try. It's been my preferred method of bed preparation ever since. It seemed like a good winter project for clearing ground as well as clearing the garage of several piles of newspaper that had somehow missed recycling day. This method is so easy a five-year-old child or an 85-year-old adult can do it without risk of injury.

Organic mulching with newspaper is a great way to kill undesirable undergrowth, or to keep shrub borders clear of weeds while a desirable groundcover takes hold. A thick layer of newspaper works by smothering out whatever it covers, from the thick trunks of poison ivy to turf grass. The papers prevent light from penetrating, making undesirable plants like turf grass and weeds die underneath. No light, no leaves. Paper allows rainfall to soak into the ground below and the warmth generated by the decomposing plant matter under the paper fosters a healthy population of earthworms that move in and aerate the soil, thus further enriching the site for healthy plant growth.

Usually it takes four to six sheets to kill grass and up to 15 sheets to kill poison ivy and woody underbrush. For heavy undergrowth, you must cut the vegetation down to the ground before laying on the newspaper; it's easy to do in the winter when plants are dormant and leafless. When selecting newspaper, use only black newsprint pages, not the glossy inserts. It helps to lay the paper down in small sections. On windy days, I keep the hose handy to spray the paper so it stays put while I work. I overlap each section generously to prevent stubborn tufts of grass and weeds from creeping through. To finish off, I top-dress the area with a thick layer of mulch that holds the paper down while decomposition takes place.

When working around lawn areas, some gardeners like to remove the outer edge of sod beforehand to maintain the integrity of the planting area. I prefer to let nature decompose the undesirables under the paper for a season or two and cut a clean edge against the lawn with a straight edged spade later. If you're in a hurry, you can have a garden in one season by laying the newspaper down over the grass, mounding a six inch layer of amended topsoil on top of the paper, planting the plants and finishing with a top dressing of mulch. Most garden annuals and perennials will scarcely know they're growing atop the grass, and decomposition will be complete the following year. The benefit from all this is that you don't have to break your back scalping grass or digging out treacherous weeds and the decomposed plant matter under the paper adds another two- or three-inch layer of good topsoil to the bed after it breaks down. The black printed sheets are entirely biodegradable, breaking down in about a year depending on the thickness. This bed-making process takes time for the turf to break down under the paper. Beds prepared in the spring are generally ready for fall planting and beds prepared in the fall are ready in the spring. It's a perfect end-of-winter project for those sunny, cool days before spring breaks into a run. While the winter rages on, undergrowth decomposes and the bed will be ready for further amendments, tilling and planting in the spring.

Soil Amendments

Okay, so now that you know the easiest way to prepare the soil, it's important to explore your options for actually enriching the soil. The turf under the newspapers will eventually break down into two or four inches of good topsoil, but you may want to give your plants an even better chance at health and survival by incorporating even more organic material into the bed. You can do this several ways—by covering the grass with organic material such as shredded leaves or compost followed by the newspapers and mulch; by mounding organic material on top of the mulch after the decomposition period and tilling or forking it all in; or by digging individual holes and enriching each hole with soil amendments after the newspaper and mulch has done its job.

Over the years I've prepared soil all three ways. When I'm short on good organic material I enrich only the soil in and around individual planting holes, but when preparing new beds, I prefer to add a layer of shredded leaves over the turf before I cover it with newspaper and mulch. The leaves act like magnets for earthworms and the decomposition process seems to go a lot faster with rich organic matter under the newspaper.

There are many types of soil enriching amendments. Some gardeners swear by cow manure, others swear by leaf mold. The goal is to add enough rich, crumbly, organic "stuff" to the earth to create a hospitable environment for new plantings and to keep adding organic material on a regular basis to keep the cycle of health moving along.

Making "Brown Gold" Naturally

For me, the best soil amendment is the compost I make in my own garden. Entire books have been written on the subject of composting, making it seem far more complicated than it really is. That's unfortunate because making compost is a cheap and reliable way to enrich garden soil and uses a lot of the biodegradable stuff you'd normally throw away or put down the garbage disposal. Also by composting at home I've recycled refuse that would have ended up composting in the landfill. It's very simple to do, and you don't have to compost by the ton for it to be effective; although many true gardeners dream of such quantities of this terrific soil amendment!

By incorporating finished compost into the soil, I've enriched the earth, attracted earthworms, broken up clay, improved drainage, aerated the soil and added important nutrients required for lush plant growth—naturally.

What most people don't realize when they're preparing a new bed is that it takes 25 to 50 percent organic material incorporated into the soil to enrich it and make a difference in plant health. That's a lot of money spent if you're buying bags of topsoil and cow manure. Compost is invariably the answer, but many people consider composting a nasty affair. They're afraid of unsightly piles of rotting material in their yards, offensive odors, rats and other vermin. Aside from one of the dogs occasionally pilfering an eggshell or two, my compost pile has never suffered any of these hazards. When you think about it, the whole earth is really just a large compost pile—constantly renewing and enriching itself with leaves, dead plants and other dead things that break down to form new soil—dust to dust.

Now that gardening has become de rigueur among the masses, a virtual flood of high-tech compost containers have appeared on the market, making it possible for the gardener to have his compost any way he likes it. He can cook it, spin it, hide it, bag it or let it rot underground. Having always preferred the simplest route, I use a no-frills bin purchased from a garden supply catalog and have it near the potting shed in the garden.

Basically, compost is the dark, rich smelling stuff that results from the decomposition of all the things you'd normally stuff down the garbage disposal, rake from the lawn or scoop from your pet rabbit or horse. My composting method is simple. I throw in a potpourri of kitchen scraps, egg shells, leaves, grass clippings, garden debris, coffee grounds, sod (roots up) and an occasional bag of horse manure from the farm down the road. I avoid meat, bones, fat, dog or cat droppings, weeds that have gone to seed, any green material treated with pesticides or fertilizers and large quantities of fresh grass clippings which tend to smell bad if not dried out and thinly layered in the compost pile. Occasionally I take a garden fork and "fluff" up the pile to add air and speed the process along. The raw materials break down in roughly two seasons, give or take.

Composting can be as simple or as complex as you like. Some gardeners enjoy aerating and turning the pile every couple of days and some, like me, look upon it as a chore. Good things come to those who wait, and I consider myself a patient composter. Those who wish for faster results must turn the contents in the compost container more frequently thus suffering more work.

In the spring and fall I load the rich, crumbly finished compost into my wheelbarrow and use it around precious specimen plants or in making new garden beds. There never seems to be enough "brown gold" to go around so it's doled out sparingly.

Other Soil Amendments

Now if the prospect of casting your biodegradables into a bin outside is just a bit too much for you, you'll have to enrich your soil with other organic materials. Because you'll need so much to make a difference, you'll want to turn to those soil amendments that you can obtain at minimal cost and effort. Many municipalities now shred leaves in the fall and offer "leaf mold" to the public for the taking. In Virginia, the county landfill shreds both leaves and tree limbs and offers huge piles of leaf mold and wood mulch for free. Leaf mold is an invaluable organic material for gardens— second only to compost. When generously worked into the soil it creates an airy, hospitable environment for plants and soil organisms. Far more economical and environmentally better than peat moss, leaf mold breaks up clay soil and increases the moisture retention of sandy soil.

If you don't have access to shredded leaves or compost you'll have to resort to buying bags of soil amendments at the local nursery or home improvement center. Topsoil, humus, loam, composted cow manure, bark fines, composted leaves and "soil conditioners" are all beneficial. Remember that you'll have to add a lot of organic matter to make a difference. One or two bags won't work for a large bed. Twenty-five percent of the bed should consist of organic material to make a difference. To be most effective, amendments should be spread on the bed and forked or tilled into the top layers of the soil. Planting can then proceed.

Planting Plants

The old adage, "Dig a hundred dollar hole for a ten dollar tree" is still true today. When preparing to plant, holes should be dug so that the plant sits at the same level that it grew in the nursery pot. Dig holes large enough for expansion—two to three times the width of the rootball and no deeper than the plant grew in the nursery. Roughen up the sides of the hole to be sure roots find their way into the surrounding ground. Small, hastily dug holes only spell disaster later. It helps to add a bit of amended soil to the bottom of the hole. Finish by filling in around the plant with soil and creating a "water well" around the perimeter where water can soak the rootball. Water the plant well and top it all off with a good layer of mulch to preserve moisture and keep weeds down.

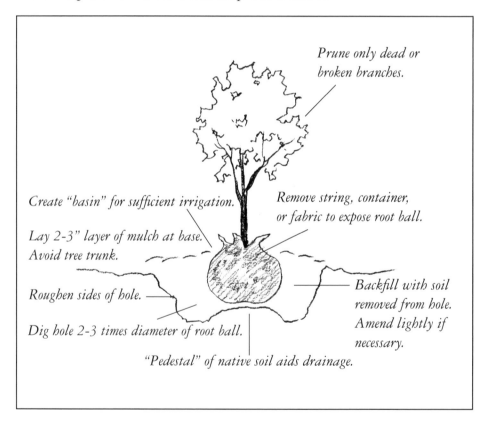

Prune only dead or broken branches.

Create "basin" for sufficient irrigation.

Lay 2-3" layer of mulch at base. Avoid tree trunk.

Remove string, container, or fabric to expose root ball.

Roughen sides of hole.

Dig hole 2-3 times diameter of root ball.

Backfill with soil removed from hole. Amend lightly if necessary.

"Pedestal" of native soil aids drainage.

Mulch

Selecting the best mulch for your garden can get confusing because there are so many types. First, it's important to understand the role of mulch in your garden. Mulch is put down to prevent weed growth, retain soil moisture, cool roots, contribute organic matter to the soil, prevent soil from splashing on leaves when it rains and improve the looks of the bed. That's a big contribution for such an ordinary garden material!

Nevertheless, mulch is an important element to maintaining plantings and eases life for many gardeners. There are many products that are called "mulch". Gravel and black plastic are a type of mulch, as are shredded bark, leaves and wood chips. The key to selecting the best mulch is to consider whether the product performs all of the duties stated above. Gravel is permanent and may never have to be laid down again, but it doesn't cool roots and contribute organic matter to the soil. Black plastic smothers weeds but doesn't contribute to soil nutrition. Shredded leaves are better composted and mixed in as a soil amendment than applied as mulch where they tend to attract slugs.

In my own garden I mulch with shredded hardwood mulch each spring. I buy it in bags which allows me to spread it a little at a time. Shredded mulch binds together, keeps weeds at bay, retains soil moisture and will not wash away. It's attractive, slowly breaks down into the soil and blends nicely with all my plants. And because the pieces of mulch actually bind together, I can use a thin layer of it to dress beds. Some nurseries offer shredded bark mulch by the yard, delivered and dumped on your driveway (or parking space!), but I've found that the mulch tends to get heavy and difficult to spread if left out in the rain. Forty-pound bags of mulch are far easier to handle for smaller gardens.

Fertilizing

We need to eat, and our plants are no different. Often students ask me about a plant that died or was "difficult to grow". After first inquiring about the soil it grew in, I ask, "Did you fertilize it?" Invariably the answer is no. Plants need three things to survive and flourish—good soil, water and food. It's that simple.

There are two types of fertilizer available: inorganic and organic. The type you choose is a personal decision because plants can't really tell the difference. Inorganic fertilizers are synthetic chemicals manufactured by man. The best are time-released products like "Osmocote", which are applied at the beginning of the growing season and slowly fertilize plants for long periods of time. Organic fertilizers are better for the environment and build healthy soil as well as feed plants, but they must be applied more frequently as part of an overall soil building effort in your garden. Whether you use one or the other depends on your level of attention to the garden, the types of plants you grow and your commitment to the environment.

You couldn't pay me to fertilize with anything other than organic products on my food plants. Somehow biting into a tomato that was fertilized with a synthetic petroleum product is just not appetizing to me. For my edibles, it's organic fertilizers all the way. I do, however, use a synthetic time-released fertilizer on the ornamental perennials that I love to grow. When properly applied, time-released fertilizers cut down on my work, don't burn plants and don't wash away into streams and waterways like non-time-released products can.

You'll notice a set of three numbers on the labels of fertilizers where you shop. These numbers indicate the "NPK ratio" or percentage of the three major nutrients that plants require for good growth—nitrogen, phosphorus and potassium. Usually you'll see three numbers like 10-10-10 or 5-10-5. The first number indicates the nitrogen content, followed by phosphorus and potassium. If you're concerned about the environment, look for products that are labeled "low analysis" or "natural organic". These fertilizers will typically have lower NPK ratio's like 1-1-1 for commercial packaged compost. No matter which type of fertilizer you use, it's important to look for a balanced or proportional set of numbers on the label like 1-1-1 or 5-10-5. This is better for your garden than 25-10-10 where the larger number indicates an excessive amount of nitrogen which causes fast green growth, but may also result in weak root systems or stems. Balanced numbers are always better.

No matter which you choose, be sure to follow all label directions; too much fertilizer can kill plants just as much as too little. Also, if you're tempted to fertilize plants with manure from horses, cows, chickens or rabbits, be sure to "age" it in a compost bin for four to six months before applying it to the garden. Fresh manure is too strong for most plants and can burn tender foliage.

Watering

Watering is one of the most enjoyable aspects of gardening. As a gardener, you'll automatically become a "weather watcher" to be sure your plants are all receiving the proper amount of moisture—from the clouds and from the end of your garden hose. Rainfall can be elusive during the height of summer, even though this is the time when tender young plants need moisture the most. It's important for plants to receive at least an inch of rainfall a week; you'll have to water if rain isn't in the forecast. Track the weather's progress, invest in a "rain gauge" or merely set a coffee can somewhere out of sight in the garden to assess the amount of rainfall the garden receives on a weekly basis. If the gauge or can contains less than an inch of rainfall, you'll need to water.

As I said earlier, well improved soil that's mulched and amended with lots of organic material holds more moisture for roots than lean soil. With rich soil you'll actually water the garden less than you would with unconditioned soil. I usually water in the morning so moisture evaporates throughout the day. This prevents mold and mildew on plants like phlox, bee balm and roses. Water whenever the plants need it though. If you arrive home from work at the end of the day and the plants in your garden are limp, water them then. They'll surely perk up by the next morning.

Container gardens should be watered daily as moisture evaporates quickly from such tight growing quarters. I irrigate containers until I see water seeping from the drainage holes in the bottom of the pot. That way I know I've moistened the soil all the way to the bottom of the pot. Always take the time to water the garden deeply rather than just giving it a quick squirt with the hose. Sparse watering promotes shallow root growth which in turn depletes the energy and vigor of plants.

Regular Care

A garden does not take care of itself. Regular care is an absolute must to keep it looking its best and prevent "nature" from taking over. You can keep chores to a minimum by providing the best growing conditions for your plants, mulching to keep weeds down, feeding and watering plants well. Good conditions promote vigorous growth which in turn requires less maintenance.

Regular chores such as removing spent blossoms, pruning broken stems, staking for strong growth and going on "weed" patrol will keep the garden looking its best. "Deadheading", or the removal of old flower blossoms, is the way I groom my flowering plants. I clip off dead flowers with shears or the pruners I always carry in my back pocket and compost them. This also gives me the opportunity to inspect each plant up close for pests.

I also regularly check plants for dead or broken stems and clip these off. With children and pets at play in the garden, a certain amount of plant damage is bound to occur and regular pruning keeps plants looking tidy. Staking too, is an absolute necessity for flower growers. I usually cut a simple tomato cage in half with a hack-saw to get two "hoops" which then get pushed into the ground around the emerging foliage of plants in the spring. The plants grow through the hoops and gain the best support for the least amount of money or effort on my part. The hoops are gathered and stored in the fall and used again the following year.

Remember to address this important chore BEFORE plants grow too large. Staking after flowers are lying on the ground always looks like.....well, staking. The trick is that you don't want the garden to look all tied and trussed up. Stakes should be discreetly hidden among foliage, hence the necessity of staking early in the season. If late season staking is necessary, support the plant with one hand while sticking a few cut tree branches around the perimeter with the other. This kind of "pea staking" looks more natural than any other attempt at support so late in the season.

Weeding

Weeding is also an important garden chore because weeds not only ruin the lovely picture we're trying to create, they weaken garden plants by stealing moisture and nutrients and eventually smothering them out. I attack weeds on my knees, pulling plants out by hand and occasionally resorting to my hand-trowel to unearth the heavier rooted specimens. It's a regular aerobic workout that's good for the body, and mind-cleansing as well.

It's best to pull weeds when they are young, and pull them after a good soaking rain. They come out of the ground more readily then; and if they haven't gone to seed, they can be added to the compost pile to rot. Weeds that have gone to seed, however, should be thrown in the garbage so their tenacious progeny cannot invade your garden again.

Pest and Disease Control

"Chemical" is a bad word among environmentally aware gardeners and for good cause. In the past few decades we've learned that synthetic insecticides and fertilizers cause more problems than they solve. Chemicals leave toxic residues in the soil, water and on plants. They kill indiscriminately—harming good organisms as well as bad. Pests can develop resistance to sprays and humans suffer from long term exposure. Nobody wins with the chemical approach.

This is where "integrated pest management" comes into play. In short, integrated pest management is the regular monitoring of pest activity in the garden to determine when, and most important, if to take action. Regular attention to your plants will enable you to catch problems early which is the best time to control insect and disease problems. By beginning with the right plants in the right places and well amended soil, the garden will be well on its way to lush healthy growth. Insects and disease prey only on weaker species and if you're providing healthy growing conditions, pest and disease problems will be minimal.

The level of chemical use in your garden will be determined, in part, by the type of garden you wish to have. Gardeners must determine what they're going for. Do you want a simple cottage garden of pretty flowers, or do you want to grow champion roses for the show table? Can you tolerate a few chewed leaves or must you have picture perfect blossoms? The answer will determine the level of chemical use in your garden.

Most gardeners want ornamental landscapes that are trouble-free. When pest or disease control is warranted, non-toxic methods of control should be tried first. This could consist of physically removing pests such as spraying aphids off plants with a heavy jet of water from the hose, picking Japanese beetles off plants or removing slugs from under boards placed around the garden. These mechanical methods help target your efforts in a safe, sane way.

In my own garden I rely on plants that are relatively pest free. This includes a long list of American native plants like purple coneflowers, coreopsis, native columbine and Virginia bluebells. More and more, our garden gives itself over to the types of plants that tolerate our climate well and remain pest free. Some special plants like hybrid nasturtiums always succumb to aphids toward the end of the summer, but not without first rewarding me with many flowers. When the aphids appear in numbers, I pull the plants out. It's that simple. Slugs that love to feast on hosta and daylily leaves find their demise at the bottom of beer laden saucers placed around the garden. Deer (our worst pest) are deterred with sprays that taste bad, but are otherwise harmless.

Biological control of garden pests can also be achieved by boosting the number of predatory insects in the garden. Golden yarrow, that most glorious perennial favorite, is a great attractor plant for these "good guy" bugs. Most chemical free gardens host large numbers of predatory insects which play an important role in the natural checks and balances of the garden. You might have aphids, but you might also have a healthy, welcome population of lady bugs that eat them. Severe damage never occurs to plants because the garden environment is diverse enough to invite predators to stay and "dine in".

Those gardeners who wish to tip the scales in their favor can release predatory insects like lady bugs, green lacewings and minute parasitic wasps into the garden. Lady bugs lay eggs on aphid infested plants, which in turn hatch into larvae that feed voraciously on aphids. Green lacewing larvae feed on aphids, mealybugs, scale, white fly, thrips, mites and spider mites. Minute trichogramma wasps feed on the eggs of cabbage worm, tomato hornworm, cutworms and an assortment of other vegetable destroying worms. Predatory insects fight pest infestations naturally, selectively and with no toxicity.

When all else fails, you might turn to pesticides, but begin with the least toxic sprays such as insecticidal soap before working up to more toxic chemicals. "Botanical insecticides" are compounds derived from plants or minerals. Unlike synthetic insecticides, botanical controls break down quickly and leave less dangerous residues in the environment. It's important to note, however, that even so called, "organic" insecticides such as rotenone, neem oil, pyrethrum, and BT (Bacillus thuringiensis) can kill beneficial insects like bees and butterflies. Target your control efforts carefully, read the label and always wear the proper safety gear when applying any pest control.

Integrated pest management doesn't provide a quick fix. It requires more planning and careful observation to catch garden pests and disease before they become a problem. It's important to be aware of what's going on in your garden and stay open to compromise. A few bad tomatoes aren't worth damaging the environment or endangering your health. Sprays will produce a flawless landscape but at the price of lifelessness in the garden. That's not really the goal for most gardeners.

The Yearly "Chores" Checklist

January
Check and clean garden tools. Replace if necessary.
Go over seed catalogs and list seeds needed for next year.
Head to the library to research garden ideas for next season.
Make a plan of the garden on paper—draw up a plant list
    to buy from in the spring.
Remove heavy snow from plants using a broom and a gentle upward
    sweeping motion. Never sweep down!
Avoid using rock salt on pavement. Use sand or kitty litter for traction
    instead.
Call landscape designers about future work now to beat
    the spring rush.

February

Remove broken branches caused by winter damage.

Prune dormant trees like maple and summer flowering
shrubs like rose of sharon and crape myrtle.

Order seeds.

Plan your garden on paper—consult local designers.

Have your soil tested.

Move trees and shrubs while still dormant.

Have lawnmower serviced. Check tire pressure.

Install trellis for vines and hang brackets for window
boxes and hanging baskets.

Inspect fence and gates for needed repairs.

Haul leaf mold from county recycling center and pile four
inches thick on new garden areas (to be tilled into
the soil in the spring).

March

Plan to attend flower and garden shows this month.

Start seeds indoors.

Keep a record of seeds started and their performance.

Seed or reseed lawn.

Fertilize trees, shrubs and lawn.

Start spring clean-up—mulch leaves, clean beds, etc.

Start a compost pile.

Prune butterfly bush and hydrangea back to ten inches.

When forsythia blooms, apply crabgrass control to lawn.

Cut ornamental grasses back to three inches.

Prune roses.

Sow annual meadow flowers.

Clean out tool shed and garage.

Clean outdoor furniture; repair if necessary.

Stake emerging perennials.

Edge ornamental beds with a straight edged spade.

April

Plant trees and shrubs.

Fertilize azaleas after they flower.

Remove tent caterpillars from affected trees.

Remove dead flowers from bulbs but let foliage wither naturally.

Make a list of bulbs to buy in autumn for bloom next spring.

Buy soil amendments for new beds.

Begin to harden off seedlings—cover with old sheet at night.

Spread newspaper and mulch on areas to be planted in autumn.

Use time-released fertilizer on all perennial and annual beds as
well as in container plantings.

Rake spent birdseed from under feeders and discard in trash.

Hang hummingbird nectar feeders.

Move emerging waterlilies to their plant shelves or onto
cinderblocks within 18" of the water's surface for the
summer.

May

Amend soil in new garden beds by forking or rototilling.

Mulch all beds after planting to keep weeds down.

Plant container gardens such as hanging baskets and
window boxes.

Plant tender vegetables after last frost.

Mow lawn at highest setting to prevent weeds in lawn.

Deadhead annuals and perennials regularly.

Install annuals after last frost date.

Clip hedges.

Turn compost pile.

Prune forsythia, lilac and azalea after blooming if necessary.

Pull weeds while still young after a rainfall.

Plug in rooted cuttings of pachysandra, periwinkle and
ajuga where groundcovers are needed.

June

Remove iris seed pods.

Install new plants throughout the month—water well.

Turn compost pile.

Make sure that container gardens are watered daily if they need it.

July

Water deeply—at least one inch a week. Use a rain gauge.

Spray hybrid roses with a fungicide to control mildew and
black spot.

Make sure containers and garden are watered during your
vacation.

Turn compost pile.

Keep watering new plants during periods of summer drought.

August
Plan a fall garden project on paper now.
Plan for fall lawn care such as reseeding, weed control and
    fertilizing now.
Continue to keep garden watered.
Freeze or can summer fruits and vegetables.
Turn compost pile.
Plan a garden pond or water feature for your yard.
Check all climbing plants to be sure they are secure on their
    supports.
Organize tool shed or garage.
Return old plastic pots and flats to the nursery for recycling.

September
Fertilize lawn at the end of the month.
Do not prune forsythia, lilac or azalea because you will
    be removing next year's flowers.
Plant trees, shrubs and other plants now. Mulch and water well.
Order spring flowering bulbs now.
Seed or reseed the lawn now.
Lime application to turf can be done during the fall. Test
    soil pH first!
Clean and restock bird feeders.
Remove seed heads from sunflowers and let dry. Put out the
    entire head for birds this winter.
Divide and move perennials now.
Take cuttings of groundcover like periwinkle and pachysandra
    to be rooted indoors over the winter.
Build large labor-intensive projects like stone walls, patios,
    ponds, walkways and retaining walls while the weather is cool.
Treat patio or decking with a wood preservative for the winter.

October
Prepare new beds and borders with newspaper and mulch.
Plant spring flowering bulbs.
Continue to install trees and shrubs.
Water recently planted trees and shrubs well.
Fertilize lawn now if you missed it last month.

Keep a record of garden successes and failures for next year.

Store outdoor cushions for the winter.

Lift half-hardy bulbs and store in perlite in a cool, dark location.

Rake and compost tree leaves.

Compost spent annuals.

Mow for the last time. Trim turf edges for a tidy appearance.

Prune yellowing waterlily plants to the crown and sink pots
   to the bottom of the pond.

Keep falling leaves out of the pond by skimming daily.

Clear vegetable and annual flower beds of summer vegetation.

Mulch beds and borders.

Install pansies for autumn color.

Take cuttings of geraniums and impatiens for indoor winter
   rooting of new plants.

Bring tender houseplants and garden plants such as geranium,
   fuchsia and herbs into the house before the first frost. Spray
   first with insecticidal soap to prevent pest infestations. Be
   sure to repot in the spring if necessary.

November

Spray newly planted evergreens such as rhododendron with
   an anti-desiccant to protect against winter damage.

Fertilize all broad-leaf evergreens such as rhododendron, holly
   and azalea now.

Fertilize shade and flowering trees now. For shade trees
   use 10-10-10 and for flowering trees use a 5-10-5 formula.

Clean out birdhouses and nesting boxes.

Take down hummingbird feeder. Clean and store.

Store all terra cotta pots indoors for the winter.

Clean out and compost all soil from hanging baskets, window
   boxes and container gardens.

December

Stock suet in suet feeders for overwintering birds.

Keep feeders filled throughout the winter.

Water newly planted trees and shrubs to prevent winter die-back.

Sources for Townhouse Gardeners

Gardening Supplies and Tools

A.M. Leonard
P.O. Box 816
Piqua, Ohio 45356
1-800-543-8955

Gardener's Eden
P.O. Box 7307
San Francisco, Ca 94120
1-800-822-9600

Gardener's Supply Company
128 Intervale Road
Burlington, VT 05401
1-800-863-1700

Langenbach
P.O. Box 1420
Lawndale, CA 90260
1-800-362-1991

Smith & Hawken
P.O. Box 6900
Florence, KY 41022
1-800-776-3336

Garden Furniture and Ornaments

Country Casual
17317 Germantown Road
Germantown, MD 20874
1-800-284-8325

Florentine Craftsmen, Inc.
46-24 28th Street
Long Island City, N.Y. 11101
1-800-876-3567

Kinsman Company
River Road
Point Pleasant, PA 18950
1-800-733-4146

Tidewater Workshop
Route 9
Oceanville, NJ 08231
1-800-666-TIDE

Winterthur Museum, Garden
and Library
Route 52
Winterthur, DE 19735
1-800-448-3883

Bulbs

Netherland Bulb Company, Inc.
13 McFadden Road
Easton, PA 18045
1-800-755-2852

The Daffodil Mart
85 Broad Street
Torrington, CT 06790
1-800-255-2852

Van Bourgondien Brothers
245 Route 109
P.O. Box 1000
Babylon, NY 11702
1-800-622-9997

Water Gardening Plants and Supplies

Lilypons Water Gardens
P.O. Box 10
Buckeystown, MD 21717
1-800-999-5454

Water Ways Nursery
13015 Milltown Road
Lovettsville, VA 22080
(540) 822-5994

Organic Gardening Products

Gardens Alive
5100 Schenley Place
Lawrenceburg, IN 47025
(812) 537-8650

Wildflower Seed Mixes

The Vermont Wildflower Farm
Reservation Center, Wildflower
   Lane
P.O. Box 1400
Louisiana, MO 63353
1-800-424-1165

Perennials, Shrubs and Other Plants

Andre Viette Farm and Nursery
Route 1, Box 16
Fisherville, VA 22939
(540) 943-2315

White Flower Farm
P.O. Box 50
Litchfield, CT 06759
1-800-503-9624

Wayside Gardens
1 Garden Lane
Hodges, SC 29695
1-800-845-1124

Jackson and Perkins
P.O. Box 1028
Medford, OR 97501
1-800-292-4769

Seeds

Park Seed Company, Inc.
1 Parkton Avenue
Greenwood, SC 29647
1-800-845-3369

Shepherd's Garden Seeds
30 Irene Street
Torrington, CT 06790
(860) 482-3638

The Cook's Garden
P.O. Box 535
Londonderry, VT 05148
1-800-457-9703

W. Atlee Burpee and Company
300 Park Avenue
Warminster, PA 18991
1-800-888-1447

Bibliography

Bier, Peg. *Townhouse Gardens Bulletin #122. Merrifield, Virginia:* Merrifield Garden Center, 1995.

Billington, Jill. *Small Gardens with Style. London:* Ward Lock, 1994.

Carney, Nancy. *Article: Mulch, Don't Dig, Fine Gardening Magazine. New town, Connecticut:* The Taunton Press, November/December, 1989.

Colborn, Nigel. *Shortcuts to Great Gardens. Boston:* Little, Brown and Company, 1993.

Larke, Stan. *Plants and Gardens in Towns and Cities. Toronto:* McGraw-Hill Ryerson Limited, 1975.

McHoy, Peter. *The Small Garden Book. New York:* Smithmark Publishers, Inc., 1995.

Murray, Elizabeth and Derek Fell. *Home Landscaping. New York:* Simon and Schuster, 1988.

Strong, Roy. *Successful Small Gardens. New York:* Rizzoli International Publications, Inc., 1995.

Tarling, Thomasina. *Truly Tiny Gardens. North Pomfret, Vermont:* Trafalgar Square Publishing, 1995.

Tarling, Thomasina. *The Container Garden. New York:* Sterling Publishing Company, Inc., 1994.

Toll, Julie. *The Wayside Garden's Collection, The Small Garden. New York:* Sterling Publishing Company, Inc., 1995.

Toogood, Alan. *Garden Illusions. Topsfield, Massachusetts:* Salem House Publishers, 1988.

Yang, Linda. *The City and Town Gardener. New York:* Random House, 1990.

Sunset's Landscaping for Small Spaces. Menlo Park, California: Sunset Publishing Corporation, 1992.

Acknowledgments

This work would never have been possible were it not for the friendship, deep support and kindness of my dear friends on (and around) Surrey House Way. I would like to thank Anne Marie Vivirito, Laura Coleman, Janice Gray, Betsy Chesky, Cheryl Godridge, Ann Sabol, Mary Brown, Deb Lesser, Jessica Grivas, Veronica Schnipple, Jeannie McElveen, Kathleen Esposito, and Cindi Munse who are simply the best neighbors and friends I could ever have. Thanks for cups of "Red Rose" tea (and stronger libations!), for last minute dinnertime "borrowing", for listening and caring, for nurturing my family, for comforting hugs and for lots and lots of wonderful laughter!

I would also like to graciously acknowledge the efforts of my publisher, Evelyn Metzger in seeing this book through to publication. Her achievements are an inspiration to all women and I am encouraged by her strength, wisdom, spirit and kindness. I also extend many thanks to the entire staff of EPM Publications, Inc. for their support. Thanks to Janet Nelson for keeping it all organized and for being a friend when I've needed a lift, and to Virginia Rosick for keeping the numbers straight and her encouragement.

I'm also grateful for the artistry and patience of Tom Huestis, this book's designer. His creative and technical talents are greatly admired and appreciated. Many thanks and praise go out to Elaine Butt as well. As the illustrator of this book, Elaine put in many hours to transform my rough ideas into beautiful and unique illustrations. I enjoyed getting to know her over many pleasant lunches and meetings. Her talent is enviable and greatly appreciated.

The designers, landscape architects and garden professionals who submitted designs for this book also merit much thanks. I'm grateful for their artistry, extensive knowledge and passion for outdoor space. Many of them took time out of their busiest spring season to meet with me and go over plans for this book. They are largely responsible for making this work unique.

I'd also like to acknowledge friends in the Pleasant Valley Writer's Group for their kind words and encouragement—-may the "publishing gods" smile upon you all.

Finally, I'd like to thank the two greatest loves of my life, my husband and our son, Jeff and Sean. They are my source of never ending loyalty, support, laughter, strength, passion, comfort, optimism, hope and love. Every day is another miracle with them.

Design and Photo Credits

(1) *A Low Maintenance Front Yard Garden:* by Sherry Mitchell

(2) *A Garden for Evening Entertainment:* by American Home Landscape, Inc., Catharpin, Virginia

(3) *A Garden for Under a Deck:* by American Home Landscape, Inc., Catharpin, Virginia

(4) *A Contemporary Garden:* Petro Design/Build, Inc., Mitchellville, Maryland

(5) *A Fragrant Side Yard Garden:* Adapted from a design by American Home Landscape, Inc., Catharpin, Virginia

(6) *A Garden for a Sling Site:* Adapted from a plan by American Home Landscape, Inc., Catharpin, Virginia

(7) *A Birdwatcher's Garden:* by Sherry Mitchell

(8) *A Garden for Hummingbirds and Butterflies:* by Sherry Mitchell

(9) An End-Unit Front Yard: by American Home Landscape, Inc., Catharpin, Virginia

(10) *A Deck-Top Garden:* by Sherry Mitchell

(11) A Tiny Townhouse Garden: Adapted from a plan by Petro Design/Build, Inc., Mitchellville, Maryland

(12) *A Shady Garden:* by American Home Landscape, Inc., Catharpin, Virginia

(13) *The KinderGarden:* by Sherry Mitchell

(14) *A Low-Maintenance Backyard Garden:* Petro Design/Build Inc., Mitchellville, Maryland

(15) *A Cottage Garden of Edibles:* Adapted from a plan by Petro Design/Build Inc., Mitchellville, Maryland

The cover photograph of Sherry Mitchell in her garden was taken by Helene Hollander Lepkowski.

All other cover photographs were taken by Sherry Mitchell at the following locations:

Top row (l) - Home of Emily Solomon, Centreville, Virginia

Middle row (r) - Windy Hill Plant Farm, Aldie, Virginia

Bottom row (l) - Merrifield Garden Center, Fairfax, Virginia

Bottom row (c) - Green Spring Gardens Park, Alexandria, Virginia

Index

About the Author

*S*herry Mitchell grew up close to nature helping out in her family's flower shop in Maryland, riding horseback in a nearby park and also serving as a wildlife rehabilitator. As a bride, Sherry lived in a townhouse for four years in the heart of Fairfax, VA, honing her gardening skills and designing gardens for small spaces. She soon became a landscape consultant and a gardening instructor for Fairfax County Adult Education.

Her first book, *Creating Sanctuary*, on how to attract songbirds, butterflies, hummingbirds and other creatures to Washington gardens was an immediate success. She became a featured speaker at the Washington Flower and Garden Show.

She also speaks and judges at garden clubs and community events. Her writing appears regularly in the *Times Community Newspapers* of Fairfax County. She is also gardening advisor for the "Cornucopia" on the World Wide Web and currently is at work on a series of naturescaping booklets for the residents of Reston, VA, a large planned community.

Mrs. Mitchell, her husband Jeffrey and their son Sean now live on a third of an acre tract near Cub Run Valley Stream Park in Centreville, VA. When she is not gardening, or reading or writing about it, she escapes with her favorite fellows on their boat, *French Connection*.

Charlestown Branch Library
179 Main Street
Charlestown, MA 02129-3208